hand-knit
your home

hand-knit your home

30 knitted projects for a modern home

MELANIE PORTER

CICO BOOKS

LONDON NEW YORK

Published in 2013 by CICO Books
An imprint of Ryland Peters & Small
519 Broadway, 5th Floor, New York NY 10012
20–21 Jockey's Fields, London WC1R 4BW
www.cicobooks.com

10 9 8 7 6 5 4 3 2 1

A CIP catalog record for this book is
available from the Library of Congress and
the British Library.

ISBN: 978-1-908862-68-6

Printed in China

Editor: Kate Haxell
Designers: Laura Woussen and Geoff Borin
Illustrators: Kuo Kang Chen, Stephen Dew,
and Kate Simunek
Photographers: Emma Mitchell and Becky
Maynes (page 100)
Stylist: Tanya Goodwin

contents

introduction

After 10 years working as a knitwear designer for a number of international fashion brands, I created a homewares brand using knitted materials to transform vintage furniture and lamps into one-off contemporary pieces. I create my own knitted fabrics for my work, because in that way I can position color and texture exactly where I want them, and where necessary I can create a hardwearing finish through felting.

Following the success of my bespoke range, new designs for cushions and accessories have followed. These products have formed the basis of the projects in this book, and have been adapted into hand-knit patterns to suit every level of knitting skill.

I am inspired and excited by the process of hand-knitting itself, and like to challenge the materials and scale used. In Hand-Knit Your Home you will find projects to be made from rope, wool, bamboo, and mohair. Each material gives a completely different feel, from the contemporary to more classic styles.

I hope that you enjoy making these projects, and feel inspired to use hand-knitting in your own home.

MELANIE PORTER

CHAPTER 1

hot ideas

Vibrant hues can be used
to make feature pieces,
or to add yet more color
to a bold interior scheme.

knitted upright chair

Update a tired chair with a new colorful cover. It's not difficult to adapt the pattern to fit any chair of a similar style, so pick yarn colors to suit your room scheme and give your own chair a new lease of life.

Skill level ✳✳

Size

Can be adjusted to fit your own chair (see page 123)

Materials

YARN

Wool yarn such as Chunky Wool from Texere—100% pure wool; approx. 120yds (110m) per 3½oz (100g) ball Quantities will depend on individual chair measurements, but as a guide:

- Cerise (A)—3½oz (100g)/120yds (110m)
- Red (B)—7oz (200g)/240yds (220m)
- Orange (C)—3½oz (100g)/120yds (110m)
- Sunshine (D)—3½oz (100g)/120yds (110m)
- Pink (E)—3½oz (100g)/120yds (110m)

NEEDLES

Pair of US 10 (6mm) knitting needles

OTHER MATERIALS

- Chair with upholstery intact
- Cable needle
- Tapestry needle
- Staple gun
- Black fabric to cover underside of chair seat

Gauge (tension)

12 sts and 20 rows to 4in (10cm) over st st using US 10 (6mm) needles

Abbreviations

C6F—cable 6 forward: slip next 3 sts onto cable needle and hold at front of work, knit next 3 sts from left-hand needle, then knit 3 sts from cable needle
See also page 124

Pattern

CHAIR SEAT

Using A, cast on required number of sts (multiple of 4).
Row 1: [K2, p2] to end.
Rows 2–16: Work every st in 2x2 rib patt as it presents.
Row 17: Cast on 10 sts, p22, k6, p to end.

Row 18: Cast on 10 sts, knit every rem st in patt as it presents.
Row 19: Work every st in patt as it presents.
Change to B.
Rows 20–22: Work every st in patt as it presents.
Row 23: P22, C6F, p to end.
Rows 24–25: Work every st in patt as it presents.
Change to C.
Rows 26–30: Work every st in patt as it presents.
Row 31: P22, C6F, p to end.
Change to D.
Rows 32–38: Work every st in patt as it presents.
Row 39: P22, C6F, p to end.
Rows 40–45: Work every st in patt as it presents.
Change to E.
Row 46: Work every st in patt as it presents.
Row 47: P22, C6F, p to end.
Rows 48–49: Work every st in patt as it presents.
Change to C.
Rows 50–52: Work every st in patt as it presents.
Change to A.

Rows 53–54: Work every st in patt as it presents.

Row 55: P22, C6F, p to end.

Rows 56–59: Work every st in patt as it presents.

Change to C.

Rows 60–62: Work every st in patt as it presents.

Change to B.

Row 63: P22, C6F, p to end.

Rows 64–70: Work every st in patt as it presents.

Row 71: P22, C6F, p to end.

Rows 72–77: Work every st in patt as it presents.

Change to E.

Row 78: Work every st in patt as it presents.

Row 79: P22, C6F, p to end.

Rows 80–83: Work every st in patt as it presents.

Change to B.

Rows 84–85: Work every st in patt as it presents.

Change to E.

Row 86: Work every st in patt as it presents.

Row 87: P22, C6F, p to end.

Row 88: Work every st in patt as it presents.

Row 89: Bind (cast) off 13 sts, knit every st in patt as it presents to last 13 sts, bind (cast) off last 13 sts.

Change to C.

Rows 90–94: Work every st in patt as it presents.

Row 95: P9, C6F, p to end.

Change to B.

Rows 96–102: Work every st in patt as it presents.

Row 103: P9, C6F, p to end.

Rows 104–105: Work every st in patt as it presents.

Rep rows 98–105 until the knitting is the required length.

Bind (cast) off.

CHAIR BACK

Using A, cast on required number of sts (multiple of 4).

Row 1: [K2, p2] to end.

Rows 2–22: Work every st in 2x2 rib patt as it presents. (This rib is for the bottom of the chair back.)

Row 23: Cast on 15 sts, p23, k6, p to end.

Row 24: Cast on 15 sts, work every st in patt as it presents to end.

Rows 25–28: Work every st in patt as it presents.

Row 29: P23, C6F, p to end.

Rows 30–32: Work every st in patt as it presents.

Change to B.

Rows 33–36: Work every st in patt as it presents.

Row 37: P23, C6F, p to end.

Rep rows 30–37 until length from row 23 is long enough to cover front of chair back (to approx. row 64).

Next row: Bind (cast) off 15 sts at start of row, work every st in patt as it presents to last 15 sts, bind (cast) off 15 sts. Rejoin yarn to rem sts on needle.

Next row: [K2, p2] to end.

Next row: Work every st in 2x2 rib patt as it presents.

Rep last row until total length is long enough to wrap fully around chair back (remembering to allow for shrinkage in felting, see page 121).

Bind (cast) off.

TO MAKE UP

● Weave in all loose ends. Wash the knit vigorously by hand, until it is felted to the desired degree (see page 121). Leave to dry.

● Follow the illustration on page 122 and use mattress stitch (see page 114) to sew up the corners of the chair seat piece. Stretch the knit over the chair seat and secure underneath with staple gun.

● Repeat with the corners of the chair back panel. Join the cast on and bound (cast) off edges and wrap the sides around the frame to fully encase the chair back. Secure with mattress stitch (see page 114).

● Cover the underneath of the seat with black fabric, turning under the edges of the fabric and overlapping the edges of the knitting; staple gun the fabric in place.

Measuring your chair
As your chair is likely to be a different size to this one, follow the instructions on page 123 to measure your own chair and adjust the pattern to fit it.

small bell lampshade

A lovely textured lampshade; make a single one for a table or bedside lamp, or hang several in different tones of a color as a group of pendant lamps. This pattern is for one shade.

Skill level ✳ ✳ ✳

Size
Approx. 6in (15cm) high with top diameter of 3½in (9cm) and bottom diameter of 8⅛in (20.5cm)

Materials
YARN
Wool yarn such as Chunky Wool from Texere—100% pure wool; approx. 120yds (110m) per 3½oz (100g) ball.
- Claret OR Cerise—approx. 3½oz (100g)/120yds (110m)

NEEDLES
Pair of US 10 (6mm) knitting needles

OTHER MATERIALS
- Lampshade 6in (15cm) high with top diameter of 3½in (9cm) and bottom diameter of 8⅛in (20.5cm) (see Resources, page 126)
- Tapestry needle
- Pins
- Sewing needle
- Sewing thread to match lampshade lining

Gauge (tension)
15 sts and 16 rows to 4in (10cm) over patt using US 10 (6mm) needles

Abbreviations
See page 124

Pattern

PANEL

(Make three)

Cast on 31 sts (beg at base of panel).

Row 1: K1, [p2, k2] to last 2 sts, p2.

Rows 2–5: Work every st in 2x2 rib patt as it presents.

Row 6: Purl.

Row 7: K1, *(k1, p1, k1) into next st, p3tog*; rep from * to * to last 2 sts, (k1, p1, k1) into next st, k1. *33 sts*

Row 8: Purl.

Row 9: K1, *p3tog, (k1, p1, k1) into next st*; rep from * to * to last 4 sts, p3tog, k1. *31 sts*

Row 10: P1, p2tog, p to last 3 sts, p2tog, p1. *29 sts*

Row 11: K1, *p3tog, (k1, p1, k1) into next st*; rep from * to * to last 4 sts, p3tog, k1. *27 sts*

Row 12: Purl.

Row 13: K1, *(k1, p1, k1) into next st, p3tog*; rep from * to * to last 2 sts, (k1, p1, k1) into next st, k1. *29 sts*

Row 14: Purl.

Row 15: K1, *p3tog, (k1, p1, k1) into next st*; rep from * to * to last 4 sts, p3tog, k1. *27 sts*

Row 16: P1, p2tog, p to last 3 sts, p2tog, p1. *25 sts*

Row 17: K1, *p3tog, (k1, p1, k1) into next st*; rep from * to * to last 4 sts, p3tog, k1. *23 sts*

Row 18: P1, p2tog, p to last 3 sts, p2tog, p1. *21 sts*

Row 19: K1, *p3tog, (k1, p1, k1) into next st*; rep from * to * to last 4 sts, p3tog, k1. *19 sts*

Row 20: P1, p2tog, p to last 3 sts, p2tog, p1. *17 sts*

Row 21: K1, *p3tog, (k1, p1, k1) into next st*; rep from * to * to last 4 sts, p3tog, k1. *15 sts*

Row 22: Purl.

Row 23: K1, *(k1, p1, k1) into next st, p3tog*; rep from * to * to last 2 sts, (k1, p1, k1) into next st, k1. *17 sts*

Row 24: Purl.

Row 25: K1, *p3tog, (k1, p1, k1) into next st*; rep from * to * to last 4 sts, p3tog, k1. *15 sts*

Row 26: P1, p2tog, p to last 3 sts, p2tog, p1. *13 sts*

Row 27: K1, *p3tog, (k1, p1, k1) into next st*; rep from * to * to last 4 sts, p3tog, k1. *11 sts*

Row 28: Purl.

Row 29: K1, [p2, k2] to last 2 sts, p2.

Row 30–33: Work every st in 2x2 rib patt as it presents.

Bind (cast) off.

TO MAKE UP

• Weave in all loose ends. Press the knitting gently following the instructions on the yarn wrapper.

• Stretch one panel over a third of the shade and hold it in place with pins pushed into the lining. Sew the side edges to the frame using the knitting yarn. Stretch the other two panels onto the remaining spaces and hold them in place with pins. Sew them to the adjacent panels using the knitting yarn.

• Finish by neatly turning the top and bottom edges of the panels over the frame and sew them to the lining using sewing thread.

The basic shade
You can buy lampshade-making kits online, but what I often do—which is even easier—is to buy a shade at a homewares store and remove the outer cover, leaving a fully lined shade.

flower vase cozy

Covering a vase with a knitted cozy is a great way to make it good-looking enough to keep on display, even when you don't have any flowers to put in it.

Skill level ✳

Size
Approx. 6in (15cm) high by 5¾in (14.5cm) diameter

Materials
YARN
Wool yarn such as Chunky Wool from Texere—100% pure wool; approx. 120yds (110m) per 3½oz (100g) ball
- Red—approx. 1¾oz (50g)/ 60yds (55m)
- Small amounts of yarn for flowers— approx. ¾oz (20g)/25yds (23m) per flower

NEEDLES
Pair of US 10 (6mm) knitting needles
H/8 (4.5mm) crochet hook

OTHER MATERIALS
- Vase measuring 6in (15cm) high by 5¾in (14.5cm) diameter (see Resources, page 126)
- Tapestry needle
- Pins

Gauge (tension)
10 sts and 22 rows to 4in (10cm) over seed (moss) stitch using US 10 (6mm) needles

Abbreviations
See page 124

Pattern
MAIN PIECE
Cast on 40 sts.
Row 1: [K1, p1] to end.
Row 2: [P1, k1] to end.
These two rows form seed (moss) stitch.
Rep rows 1–2, 18 more times. *38 rows in total*
Bind (cast) off.

CROCHET BASE
(Note that these are US crochet terms: turn to page 116 for UK equivalents.)
Ch2.
Round 1: 12dc in 2nd ch from hook, sl st in 1st dc to join.
Round 2: Ch1, 2dc in every dc in round, sl st in 1st dc to join. *24 dc*
Round 3: Ch1, 2dc in every dc in round, sl st in 1st dc to join. *48 dc*
Round 4: Ch1, 1dc in every dc in round, sl st in 1st dc to join.
Fasten off.

FLOWERS
Following Corsage Coat Hook flower pattern (see page 20), make three flowers in a selection of colors from your yarn stash.

TO MAKE UP
- Weave in all loose ends. Press the knitting gently following the instructions on the yarn wrapper.
- Sew side seam of the main piece using mattress stitch (see page 114) to create a knitted tube. With wrong side facing out, slip the cozy over the vase and pin on the crochet base. Using overcast stitch, sew on the base.
- Turn the cozy right side out and sew on the crochet flowers with the tapestry needle and matching yarn.

Adding flowers
You can leave the vase cozy as it is, add crochet flowers—as many as you wish—or if crochet isn't your thing, sew on fabric flowers.

rope knit basket

I like to experiment with knitting using unlikely materials. Using rope with giant knitting needles is a very simple way to create a truly interesting piece that's also very functional.

Skill level ✳

Size
Approx. 10½in (27cm) high by 15¼in (38cm) wide

Materials
YARN
Cotton rope available from hardware stores
- ⅜in (10mm) thick yellow rope with core (A)—approx. 44yds (40m)
- ½in (12mm) thick black rope without core (B)—approx. 16½yds (15m)

NEEDLES
Pair of 1½in (4cm) knitting needles (see Resources, page 126)

OTHER MATERIALS
- Two 12in (30cm) basket bases (see Resources, page 126)
- Wood glue
- Black wood stain (optional)
- Two 82in (210cm) black bootlaces to attach base
- Sewing needle
- Sewing thread to match rope

Gauge (tension)
2 sts and 3 rows to 4in (10cm) over st st using 1½in (4cm) needles

Abbreviations
See page 124

Pattern
MAIN PIECE
Using A, cast on 27 sts.
Row 1: Purl.
Row 2: Knit.
These 2 rows form st st.
Work 3 more rows in st st.
Change to B.
Row 6: Knit.
Row 7: Purl.
Bind (cast) off.

BASE
- To increase the strength of the basket base I glued two base pieces together (ensuring that the holes were aligned so that they could still be used). I also stained the base black with wood stain.

TO MAKE UP
- Use matching rope to lace up the side seam. Bind the ends of the rope with matching sewing thread and sew them down on the inside of the basket.
- Using the bootlaces, lace the base onto the bottom of the basket. Secure the laces with a knot.

Choosing rope
Rope comes with or without an internal core. The core creates a stiff rope, which is heavier (and more expensive) and works well for creating a strong basket.

corsage coat hook

These pretty crochet flowers are such a super-simple way to add color and style to a traditional coat hook that you'll want to make one for every hook in the house.

Skill level ✳ ✳

Size
Approx. 4¾in (12cm) across

Materials
YARN
Wool yarn such as Chunky Wool from Texere—100% pure wool; approx. 120yds (110m) per 3½oz (100g) ball
- Orange, Sunshine, OR Ecru— approx. ¾oz (20g)/25yds (23m) per flower

HOOK
H/8 (4.5mm) crochet hook

OTHER MATERIALS
- Traditional metal coat and hat hook
- Tapestry needle

Gauge (tension)
A specific gauge is not needed for this project.

Abbreviations
See page 124

Pattern
MAIN PIECE
(Note that these are US crochet terms: turn to page 116 for UK equivalents.)
Ch26.
Row 1: Ch1, 2dc in next ch, 2dc in each ch to end. *52 dc*
Row 2: [Ch3, 1sc in 4th dc] to end.
Row 3: (1sc, 3dc, 1sc) in each of first 3 ch spaces, (1sc, 1dc, 3tr, 1dc, 1sc) in rem ch spaces. *13 petals*
Fasten off.

TO MAKE UP
- Curl into a flower shape, with the smallest petals in the center, and use matching yarn to overcast stitch the layers together on the back of the flower to secure the shape. Attach the flower to the coat hook by passing the hook through the spaces in the petals.

stash busting
This is a perfect project to use up scrap yarn. Each flower takes approximately 25yds (23m) of yarn.

cable doorstop

A lovely little weighted doorstop to add a bit of color and style to your home. Make several to match different rooms, using scraps of fabrics to match other soft furnishings for a truly coordinated look.

Skill level ✳ ✳ ✳

Size
Approx. 7in (18cm) high by 4in (10cm) wide

Materials
YARN
Wool yarn such as Chunky Wool from Texere—100% pure wool; approx. 120yds (110m) per 3½oz (100g) ball
- Sunshine—approx. 2¾oz (80g)/96yds (88m)

NEEDLES
Set of US 10 (6mm) double-pointed needles

OTHER MATERIALS
- Large cable needle
- Two 4¾in (12cm) diameter circles of fabric for the ends
- Muslin (calico) or similar fabric for lining; one piece measuring 14 x 8in (35 x 20cm) and two 4¾in (12cm) diameter circles of fabric for the ends
- Dried beans to fill
- Sewing needle
- Sewing thread
- Sewing machine

Gauge (tension)
12 sts and 17 rows to 4in (10cm) over patt using US 10 (6mm) needles

Abbreviations
C6F—cable 6 forward: slip next 3 sts onto cable needle and hold at front of work, knit next 3 sts from left-hand needle, then knit 3 sts from cable needle. See also page 124

Pattern
MAIN PIECE
Cast on 48 sts.
Evenly distribute sts over 3 or 4 double-pointed needles.
Rounds 1–6: [P1, k2, p2, k6, p2, k2, p1] 3 times.
Round 7: [P1, k2, p2, C6F, p2, k2, p1] 3 times.
Rounds 8–13: [P1, k2, p2, k6, p2, k2, p1] three times.
Rep rounds 1–13, 3 more times.
Bind (cast) off.

TO MAKE UP
- Weave in all loose ends. Wash the knit vigorously by hand until it is slightly felted (see page 121). Leave to dry.
- Taking ⅜in (1cm) seam allowances throughout, sew the short edges of the main lining piece together to form a tube. Sew one lining circle to one end. Fill the tube with dried beans and hand-sew the second circle to the other end of the tube with backstitch.
- Slip the knitted tube over the stuffed lining. Turn under the edges of the fabric circles and slipstitch on in place at each end of the knitted tube.

Choosing fabric
I've used vintage floral fabric for the ends of this doorstop, but a plain color or striped fabric would work equally well.

draft excluder

Keep the drafts out with this felted draft excluder. The cable pattern has a short repeat, so you'll pick up the rhythm very quickly, and just keep going round and round until the excluder is the right length.

Skill level ✳ ✳ ✳

Size
Approx. 30¾in (78cm) long x 4in (10cm) wide

Materials
YARN
Wool yarn such as Chunky Wool from Texere—100% pure wool; approx. 120yds (110m) per 3½oz (100g) ball
- Orange—approx. 12¼oz (350g)/420yds (385m)

NEEDLES
Set of US 10 (6mm) double-pointed needles

OTHER MATERIALS
- Large cable needle
- Two 4¾in (12cm) diameter circles of fabric for the ends
- Muslin (calico) or similar fabric for lining; one piece measuring 31½ x 14in (80 x 35cm) and two 4¾in (12cm) diameter circles of fabric for the ends
- Polyester stuffing

- Sewing needle
- Sewing thread

Gauge (tension)
12 sts and 17 rows to 4in (10cm) over patt using US 10 (6mm) needles

Abbreviations
C6F—cable 6 forward: slip next 3 sts onto cable needle and hold at front of work, knit next 3 sts from left-hand needle, then knit 3 sts from cable needle. See also page 124

Pattern
MAIN PIECE
Cast on 48 sts.
Evenly distribute sts over 3 or 4 double-pointed needles.
Rounds 1–6: [P1, k2, p2, k6, p2, k2, p1] 3 times.
Round 7: [P1, k2, p2, C6F, p2, k2, p1] 3 times.
Rounds 8–13: [P1, k2, p2, k6, p2, k2, p1] three times.
Rep rounds 1–13, 14 more times.
Bind (cast) off.

TO MAKE UP
- Weave in all loose ends. Wash the knit vigorously by hand until it is slightly felted (see page 121). Leave to dry.
- Taking ⅜in (1cm) seam allowances throughout, sew the long edges of the main lining piece together to form a tube. Sew one lining circle to one end. Fill the tube with polyester stuffing and hand-sew the second circle to the other end of the tube with backstitch.
- Slip the knitted tube over the stuffed lining. Turn under the edges of the fabric circles and slipstitch on in place at each end of the knitted tube.

Going in circles
This pattern involves knitting in the round, so if you've not done this before, turn to page 113 for instructions.

stripe knit clock

My knitted clocks are always popular as they are such a fun and unusual way to use knit in the home. The mechanisms are widely available in craft and hobby stores and online.

Skill level ✳ ✳

Size
10in (25cm) diameter

Materials

YARN

Wool yarn such as Chunky Wool from Texere—100% pure wool; approx. 120yds (110m) per 3½oz (100g) ball
- Red (A)—approx. ½oz (15g)/ 18yds (16.5m)
- Pink (B)—approx. ½oz (15g)/ 18yds (16.5m)
- Orange (C)—approx. ½oz (15g)/18yds (16.5m)
- Sunshine (D)—approx. ¼oz (12g)/14½yds (13m)
- Claret (E)—approx. ¼oz (12g)/14½yds (13m)

NEEDLES

Pair of US 10 (6mm) knitting needles

OTHER MATERIALS
- 10in (25cm) diameter cardboard cake board
- Craft knife
- 11 x 11in (28 x 28cm) of thin foam
- Scissors
- Craft glue
- Quartz clock mechanism (see Resources, page 126)
- 10 x 10in (25 x 25cm) of fabric for the back
- String
- Tapestry needle
- Sewing needle
- Sewing thread

Gauge (tension)
12 sts and 17 rows to 4in (10cm) over st st using US 10 (6mm) needles

Abbreviations
See page 124

Pattern
MAIN PIECE

Using A, cast on 20 sts.

Row 1 (RS): Knit.

Row 2: Purl.

Rep rows 1–2 once more.

Row 5: K1, inc, k to last 2 sts, inc, k1.
22 sts

Row 6: Purl.

Rep rows 5–6 twice more. *26 sts*

Change to B.

Row 11: K1, inc, [k1, p1] to last 2 sts, inc, k1. *28 sts*

Row 12: [K1, p1] to end.

Row 13: K1, inc, [p1, k1] to last 2 sts, inc, k1. *30 sts*

Row 14: [P1, k1] to end.

Change to A.

Row 15: K1, inc, k to last 2 sts, inc, k1.
32 sts

Row 16: Purl.

Rep rows 15–16 twice more. *36 sts*

Change to B.

Row 21: K1, inc, [k1, p1] to last 2 sts, inc, k1. *38 sts*

Row 22: [K1, p1] to end.

Row 23: K1, inc, [p1, k1] to last 2 sts, inc, k1. *40 sts*

Row 24: [P1, k1] to end.

Change to A.

Row 25: K1, inc, k to last 2 sts, inc, k1.
42 sts

Row 26: Purl.

Rep rows 25–26 twice more. *46 sts*

Change to C.

Row 31: Purl.

Row 32: Knit.

Rep rows 31–32 twice more.

Change to D.

Knit 2 rows.

Change to B.

Row 39: K1, p2tog, [k1, p1] to last 3 sts, k2tog, p1. *44 sts*

Row 40: [P1, k1] to end.

Row 41: P1, k2tog, [p1, k1] to last 3 sts, p2tog, k1. *42 sts*

Row 42: [K1, p1] to end.

Change to E.

Row 43: K1, k2tog, [p2, k2] to last 3 sts, p2tog, p1. *40 sts*

Row 44: Work every st in 2x2 rib patt as it presents.

Row 45: K1, p2tog, p1, [k2, p2] to last 4 sts, k1, k2tog, p1. *38 sts*

Row 46: Work every st in 2x2 rib patt as it presents.

Row 47: K1, p2tog, [k2, p2] to last 3 sts, k2tog, p1. *36 sts*

Row 48: Work every st in 2x2 rib patt as it presents.

Change to A.

Row 49: K1, k2tog, k to last 3 sts, k2tog, k1. *34 sts*

Row 50: Purl.

Rep rows 49–50, 3 more times. *28 sts*

Change to D.

Row 57: K1, k2tog, k to last 3 sts, k2tog, k1. *26 sts*

Row 58: Knit.

Rep rows 57–58, 3 more times. *20 sts*

Knit 2 rows.

Bind (cast) off.

TO MAKE UP

- Weave in all loose ends. Wash the knit vigorously by hand until it is slightly felted (see page 121). Leave to dry.
- Carefully use the craft knife to cut a ¼in (0.5cm) hole in the center of the board. Cut the foam into a circle 1in (2.5cm) larger than the cake board and wrap it over the edge, gluing it in place on the back.
- Using a running stitch, lace a strong string around the edge of the knitting. Stretch the knitting over the front of the covered board, then pull the string tight on the back and secure it with a firm double knot.
- Cut the fabric into a circle the same size as the clock. Turn under the edge by ⅜in (1cm) all around. Sew the fabric in place, covering the edge of the knitting, with sewing thread and hemming stitch.
- Cut a small hole in the backing fabric and attach the clock mechanism through the hole in the board, following the manufacturer's instructions.

Functional felting
I like to over-wash and slightly felt the knitting in order to create a less holey fabric.

color block footstool

Reinvent a traditional footstool with a contemporary pattern in bold colors. It's easy to adapt this pattern to fit a different-sized square or rectangular footstool, and very easy indeed to fit the new cover onto the stool.

Skill level ✳ ✳

Size

Can be adjusted to fit your own footstool (see page 123)

Materials

YARN

Wool yarn such as Chunky Wool from Texere—100% pure wool; approx. 120yds (110m) per 3½oz (100g) ball

- Red (A)—approx. 1¾oz (50g)/ 60yds (55m)
- Cerise (B)—approx. 1½oz (40g)/ 48yds (44m)
- Orange (C)—approx. 2¼oz (60g)/ 72yds (44m)
- Sunshine (D)—approx. 1¾oz (50g)/ 60yds (55m)

NEEDLES

Pair of US 10 (6mm) knitting needles

OTHER MATERIALS

- Large cable needle
- Footstool measuring 15 x 11½ x 4in (38 x 29 x 10cm) (see Resources, page 126)
- Tapestry needle
- 35in (90cm) of hook-and-loop tape
- Sewing needle
- Sewing thread

Gauge (tension)

12 sts and 17 rows to 4in (10cm) over st st using US 10 (6mm) needles

Abbreviations

C6F—cable 6 forward: slip next 3 sts onto cable needle and hold at front of work, knit next 3 sts from left-hand needle, then knit 3 sts from cable needle. See also page 124

Pattern

MAIN PIECE

Using A, cast on 40 sts.

Row 1 (WS): [K2, p2] to end.

Rows 2–41: Work every st in 2x2 rib patt as it presents.

Change to B.

Row 42 (RS): Purl.

Row 43: Knit.

Rep rows 42–43 once more.

Change to C.

Row 46: [P2, k6, p2] 4 times.

Rows 47–51: Work every st in patt as it presents.

Row 52: P2, C6F, p4, k6, p4, C6F, p4, k6, p2.

Rows 53–57: Work every st in patt as it presents.

Row 58: P2, k6, p4, C6F, p4, k6, p4, C6F, p2.

Rows 59–63: Work every st in patt as it presents.

Row 64: P2, C6F, p4, k6, p4, C6F, p4, k6, p2.

Rows 65–69: Work every st in patt as it presents.

Row 70: P2, k6, p4, C6F, p4, k6, p4, C6F, p2.

Rows 71–75: Work every st in patt as it presents.

Change to B.

Row 76: Purl.

Row 77: Knit.

Rep rows 76–77 once more.

Change to D.

Row 80: [K2, p2] to end.

Rows 81–120: Work every st in 2x2 rib patt as it presents.

Bind (cast) off.

FIRST SIDE PANEL

Using B, with RS facing and beg 5in (13cm) from bound (cast) off edge, pick up 44 sts down one side, ending 5in (13cm) from cast on edge—these 5in (13cm) free sections will be used to create the corner seam.

Row 1: [K2, p2] to end.

Rows 2–28: Work every st in 2x2 rib patt as it presents.

Bind (cast) off.

SECOND SIDE PANEL

Using C, with RS facing and beg 5in (13cm) from cast on edge, pick up 44 sts down the other side, ending 5in (13cm) from bound (cast) off edge— these 5in (13cm) free sections will be used to create the corner seam.

Row 1: [K2, p2] to end.

Rows 2–28: Work every st in 2x2 rib patt as it presents.

Bind (cast) off.

TO MAKE UP

- Using mattress stitch (see page 114), sew the corner seams closed to create a box shape (see page 122).
- Weave in all loose ends. Wash the knit vigorously by hand until it is felted to the desired degree (see page 121). Leave to dry.
- Hand sew strips of the hook side of the hook-and-loop tape to the underside of the footstool along each side. Pull the knitted cover over the footstool and press the knitting onto the hook-and-loop tape.

Functional felting
slightly felting the knit will create a more hardwearing cover, and the stitches won't snag when you put your feet up.

heart pillow

show your soft side with a love heart pillow. I've chosen classic pinks for my hearts, but two shades of your favorite color will look just as good, and the hearts are great stash busters as they only require a little yarn each.

Skill level ✳ ✳

Size

16 x 16in (40 x 40cm)

Materials

YARN

Wool yarn such as Chunky Wool from Texere—100% pure wool; approx. 120yds (110m) per 3½oz (100g) ball

- Ecru (A)—approx. 2¾oz (80g)/96yds (88m)
- Pink (B)—approx. ¼oz (10g)/ 12yds (11m)
- Cerise (C)—approx. ⅛oz (5g)/ 6yds (5.5m)

NEEDLES

Pair of US 10 (6mm) knitting needles

OTHER MATERIALS

- 16 x 16in (40 x 40cm) pillow pad
- Tapestry needle
- Fabric for back of pillow
- Pins
- Sewing needle
- Sewing thread
- Sewing machine

Gauge (tension)

12 sts and 17 rows to 4in (10cm) over st st using US 10 (6mm) needles

Abbreviations

Turn—turn the knitting as though you have completed the row.
See also page 124

Pattern

MAIN PIECE

Using A, cast on 58 sts.

Row 1: Knit.

Row 2: Purl.

These two rows form st st.

Work in st st until fabric measures 16½in (42cm) from cast on edge.

Bind (cast) off.

HEART

(Make two in pink and one in cerise)

Cast on 2 sts.

Row 1: K1, m1, k1. *3 sts*

Row 2 and every alt row: Purl.

Row 3: K1, m1, k1, m1, k1. *5 sts*

Row 5: K2, m1, k1, m1, k2. *7 sts*

Row 7: K3, m1, k1, m1, k3. *9 sts*

Row 9: K4, m1, k1, m1, k4. *11 sts*

Row 11: K5, m1, k1, m1, k5. *13 sts*

Row 13: K6, k1 in back loop of st below next st then k1 in next st, k6. *14 sts*

Row 15: Ssk, k3, k2tog, turn.

Cont on these 5 sts and leave rem 7 sts on needle.

Row 17: Ssk, k1, k2tog. *3 sts*

Row 18: P3tog and fasten off.

With RS facing, rejoin yarn to rem 7 sts.

Next row: Ssk, k3, k2tog. *5 sts*

Next row: Purl.

Next row: Ssk, k1, k2tog. *3 sts*

Next row: P3tog and fasten off.

TO MAKE UP

- Weave in all loose ends.
- Sew the hearts to the cushion base by sewing around the edges using matching yarn, ensuring that the heart is completely flat. Follow the photograph for position.
- Wash the knit vigorously by hand until it is slightly felted (see page 121). Leave to dry.
- Cut the fabric ⅜in (1cm) larger than the knitted panel to allow for fraying.
- Right sides together, pin the fabric to the knitted panel. Taking a ⅝in (1.5cm) seam allowance on the knitted panel, sew around three sides using a sewing machine, or by hand using backstitch.
- Turn cover right side out and insert pillow pad. Hand-sew final side closed with slipstitch.

sewing on hearts
sewing separately knitted hearts to the pillow cover—instead of working them in intarsia—gives a raised effect, which is accentuated when the knitting is washed.

CHAPTER 2

cool
collection

Calm tones can still add color; choose fresh greens and teal blues to create eye-catching accents.

color block lampshade

Using a wool/alpaca yarn to create a cover for a lampshade means that the light highlights even the finest fibers.

Skill level ✳ ✳

Size

6in (15cm) high with top diameter of 3½in (9cm) and bottom diameter of 8⅛in (20.5cm)

Materials

YARN

Wool/alpaca yarn such as Creative Focus Worsted from Rowan—75% wool, 25% alpaca; approx. 220yds (200m) per 3½oz (100g) ball
- New Fern (A)—approx. ¾oz (20g)/ 44yds (40m)
- Teal (B)—approx. ¾oz (20g)/ 44yds (40m)
- Basil (C)—approx. ¾oz (20g)/ 44yds (40m)

NEEDLES

Pair of US 6 (4mm) knitting needles

OTHER MATERIALS
- Lampshade 6in (15cm) high with top diameter of 3½in (9cm) and bottom diameter of 8⅛in (20.5cm) (see Resources, page 126)
- Tapestry needle
- Pins
- Sewing needle
- Sewing thread to match lampshade lining

Gauge (tension)

19 sts and 22 rows to 4in (10cm) over st st using US 6 (4mm) needles

Abbreviations

See page 124

Color sequence

Panel 1: Work in A throughout.
Panel 2: Cast on in A, change to B on row 9.
Panel 3: Cast on in C, change to A on row 28.
Panel 4: Cast on in C, change to A on row 10, change to B on row 14.
Panel 5: Cast on in C, change to A on row 14, change to C on row 22.
Panel 6: Cast on in B, change to C on row 16.

Pattern

PANEL

(Make six in colors as listed on page 38)
Cast on 20 sts.

Row 1: [K2, p2] to end.

Rows 2–6: Work every st in 2x2 rib patt as it presents.

Row 7: K1, p2tog, p1, [k2, p2] 3 times, k1, k2tog, p1. *18 sts*

Row 8: K1, [p2, k2] to last st, p1.

Row 9: K1, p2tog, [k2, p2] 3 times, k2tog, p1. *16 sts*

Beg with a k row, work 3 rows st st.

Row 13: P1, p2tog, p10, p2tog, p1. *14 sts*

Beg with a k row, work 3 rows st st.

Row 17: P1, p2tog, p8, p2tog, p1. *12 sts*

Beg with a k row, work 5 rows st st.

Row 23: P1, p2tog, p6, p2tog, p1. *10 sts*

Beg with a k row, work 7 rows st st.

Row 31: P1, p2tog, p4, p2tog, p1. *8 sts*

Beg with a k row, work 6 rows st st.

Row 38: [K2, p2] to end.

Rows 39–42: Work every st in 2x2 rib patt as it presents.

Bind (cast) off.

TO MAKE UP

- Weave in all loose ends. Press the knitting gently following the instructions on the yarn wrapper.
- Stretch panels one, three, and five over alternate spaces on the shade and hold it in place with pins pushed into the lining. Sew the side edges to the frame using the knitting yarn. Stretch the other remaining panels over the remaining spaces and hold them in place with pins. Sew them to the adjacent panels using the knitting yarn.
- Finish by neatly turning the top and bottom edges of the panels over the frame and sew them to the lining using sewing thread.

The basic shade
You can buy lampshade-making kits online—but what I often do, which is even easier, is to buy a shade at a homewares store and remove the outer cover, leaving a fully lined shade.

stripe drum lampshade

This knitted lampshade can be used with a knitted lampstand (see page 44), or it looks equally chic on a wooden stand painted to complement your yarn colors.

Skill level ✳ ✳

Size
9in (23cm) high and 12in (30cm) in diameter

Materials
YARN
Wool/alpaca yarn such as Creative Focus Worsted from Rowan—75% wool, 25% alpaca; approx. 220yds (200m) per 3½oz (100g) ball
- Basil (A)—approx. 1¾oz (50g)/ 110yds (100m)
- Golden Heather (B)—approx. 1¾oz (50g)/110yds (100m)
- New Fern (C)—approx. 1¾oz (50g)/ 110yds (100m)
- Natural (D)—approx. 1¾oz (50g)/ 110yds (100m)
- Cobalt (E)—approx. 1¾oz (50g)/ 110yds (100m)
- Teal (F)—approx. 1¾oz (50g)/ 110yds (100m)

NEEDLES
Pair of US 7 (4.5mm) knitting needles

OTHER MATERIALS
- Drum lampshade measuring 9in (23cm) high with a 12in (30cm) diameter (see Resources, page 126)
- Sewing needle
- Sewing thread

Gauge (tension)
19 sts and 24 rows to 4in (10cm) over st st using US 7 (4.5mm) needles

Abbreviations
See page 124

Pattern

MAIN PIECE

Using A, cast on 46 sts.

Row 1: [K2, p2] to last 2 sts, k2.

Rows 2–22: Work every st in 2x2 rib patt as it presents.

Change to B.

Row 23: [K2, p2] to last 2 sts, k2.

Rows 24–26: Work every st in 2x2 rib patt as it presents.

Change to C.

Rows 27–45: Purl.

Change to D.

Row 46: [K2, p2] to last 2 sts, k2.

Row 47: [P2, k2] to last 2 sts, p2.

Row 48: As row 47.

Row 49: As row 46.

Rep rows 46–49 once more, then work rows 46 and 47 once more.

Change to E.

Row 56: Purl.

Row 57: K1, *(k1, p1, k1) into next st, p3tog*; rep from * to * to last st, k1.

Row 58: Purl.

Row 59: K1, *p3tog, (k1, p1, k1) into next st*; rep from * to * to last st, k1.

Rep rows 56–59, 4 more times.

Change to F.

Row 76: Knit.

Row 77: Purl.

Rep rows 76–77, 9 more times.

Change to C.

Row 96: P2, [k1, p3] to end.

Row 97: [K3, p1] to last 2 sts, k2.

Rep rows 96–97, 5 more times.

Change to A.

Row 108: [Insert RH knitwise needle into next st on LH needle, wind yarn twice around the needle and k1] to end.

Row 109: Purl, working into the 1st loop of each st and allowing the extra loop to slip off the needle to its full length.

Row 110: Purl.

Row 111: Purl.

Rep rows 108–111 twice more, then rep rows 108–109 once more.

Change to F.

Row 122: Purl.

Row 123: Purl.

Row 124: [Insert RH knitwise needle into next st on LH needle, wind yarn twice around the needle and k1] to end.

Row 125: Purl, working into the 1st loop of each st and allowing the extra loop to slip off the needle to its full length.

Rep rows 122–125 once more.

Change to B.

Rows 130–149: Rep rows 56–75.

Change to D.

Rows 150–157: Purl.

Row 158: Knit.

Row 159: Purl.

Rep rows 158–159 once more.

Change to C.

Rows 162–173: Rep rows 96–107.

Change to A.

Rows 174–187: Rep rows 108–121.

Change to F.

Rows 188–195: Rep rows 122–129.

Bind (cast) off.

TO MAKE UP

• Weave in all loose ends. Press the knitting gently following the instructions on the yarn wrapper.

• Using mattress stitch (see page 114), join the cast on and bound (cast) off ends. Right side out, stretch the knitted tube over the lampshade. Neatly turn the top and bottom edges over the frame and sew them to the lining using sewing thread.

The basic shade
You can buy lampshade-making kits online—but what I often do, which is even easier, is to buy a shade at a homewares store and remove the outer cover, leaving a fully lined shade.

stripe lampstand

Update a vintage lampstand by covering it in knit. As long as the turned shapes don't go in and out too much, the knitting will stretch and contract to fit them without you having to increase or decrease stitches.

Skill level   ✳✳

Size

Can be adjusted to fit your own lampstand (see page 46)

Materials

YARN

Wool/alpaca yarn such as Creative Focus Worsted from Rowan—75% wool, 25% alpaca; approx. 220yds (200m) per 3½oz (100g) ball

- Basil (A)—approx. 3½oz (100g)/ 220yds (200m)
- New Fern (B)—approx. ½oz (15g)/ 33yds (30m)
- Teal (C)—approx. ½oz (15g)/ 33yds (30m)
- Golden Heather (D)—approx. ½oz (15g)/33yds (30m)
- Natural (E)—approx. ½oz (15g)/ 33yds (30m)
- Cobalt (F)—approx. ½oz (15g)/ 33yds (30m)

NEEDLES

Pair of US 7 (4.5mm) knitting needles

OTHER MATERIALS

- Vintage lampstand approx. 58in (145cm) tall and 6¼in (16cm) circumference, with base up to 15¼in (38cm) circumference
- Circle of fabric to cover bottom of base, cut ¾in (2cm) larger than base
- Tapestry needle
- Sewing needle
- Sewing thread to match base fabric
- Buttonhole thread

Gauge (tension)

19 sts and 24 rows to 4in (10cm) over st st using US 7 (4.5mm) needles

Abbreviations

See page 124

Pattern

BASE

Using A, cast on 259 sts.

Row 1 and every alt row: Purl.
Row 2: K2tog, k40, [sk2po, k40] 5 times, skpo. *247 sts*
Row 4: K2tog, k38, [sk2po, k38] 5 times, skpo. *235 sts*
Row 6: K2tog, k36 [sk2po, k36] 5 times, skpo. *223 sts*
Row 8: K2tog, k34, [sk2po, k34] 5 times, skpo. *211 sts*
Row 10: K2tog, K32, [sk2po, k32] 5 times, skpo. *199 sts*
Row 12: K2tog, k30, [sk2po, k30] 5 times, skpo. *187 sts*

Vintage lights
If you can hunt down a vintage lampstand with a nice shape, it's a good idea to get it re-wired by a qualified electrician.

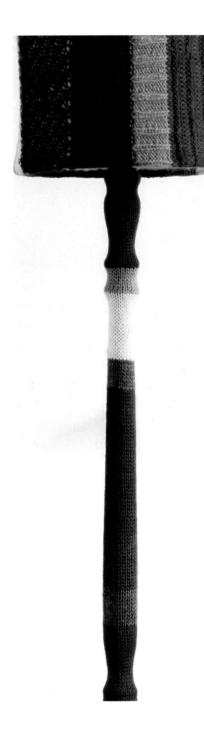

Row 14: K2tog, k28, [sk2po, k28] 5 times, skpo. *175 sts*

Row 16: K2tog, k26, [sk2po, k26] 5 times, skpo. *163 sts*

Row 18: K2tog, k24, [sk2po, k24] 5 times, skpo. *151 sts*

Row 20: K2tog, k22, [sk2po, k22] 5 times, skpo. *139 sts*

Row 22: K2tog, k20, [sk2po, k20] 5 times, skpo. *127 sts*

Row 24: K2tog, k18, [sk2po, k18] 5 times, skpo. *115 sts*

Row 26: K2tog, k16, [sk2po, k16] 5 times, skpo. *103 sts*

Row 28: K2tog, k14, [sk2po, k14] 5 times, skpo. *91 sts*

Row 30: K2tog, k12, [sk2po, k12] 5 times, skpo. *79 sts*

Row 32: K2tog, k10, [sk2po, k10] 5 times, skpo. *67 sts*

Row 34: K2tog, k8, [sk2po, k8] 5 times, skpo. *55 sts*

Row 36: K2tog, k6, [sk2po, k6] 5 times, skpo. *43 sts*

Row 38: K2tog, k4, [sk2po, k4] 5 times, skpo. *31 sts*

Bind (cast) off.

Do not join the seam on the knitted hexagon at this stage.

STAND

Using A, cast on 22 sts (starting at base).

Row 1: Knit.

Row 2: Purl.

These two rows form st st.

Cont in st st, changing colors as listed.

30 more rows in A.

10 rows in B.

10 rows in A.

18 rows in C.

4 rows in D.

30 rows in B.

8 rows in E.

14 rows in B.

8 rows in E.

10 rows in B.

24 rows in F.

10 rows in D.

16 rows in A.

40 rows in C.

8 rows in D.

20 rows in E.

8 rows in B.

34 rows in F.

At this stage, measure the knitting and pole of your lampstand; the knitting should be ¾in (2cm) longer than the pole. Add a few more rows of knitting if required.

Bind (cast) off.

TO MAKE UP

- Weave in all loose ends. Press the knitting gently following the instructions on the yarn wrapper.
- Remove the feet from the base of the stand and set them aside.
- Wrap the knitted striped piece around the pole of the lampstand and, starting at the bottom, sew the side seam using mattress stitch (see page 114). Sew up the first ¾in (2cm), then ruche that down and sew up the rest of the seam. Around narrower parts of the pole you might need to increase the seam allowance to keep the knitting tight. Gather the top edge at the top of the pole and secure it with backstitches.
- Lay the knitted base over the lamp base and close the hexagon seam using mattress stitch. Using running stitches, sew a length of buttonhole thread around the outer edge of the knitted base. Stretch the knitting over the base and draw it tight by pulling up the thread on the underside of the base. Knot the thread securely.

- Cut a very small hole in the center of the fabric circle and pass the electric cable that comes out of the lampstand base through this. Turn under the edges of the fabric by ¾in (2cm) all around. Using sewing thread and hemming stitch, sew the fabric in place, overlapping the edge of the knitting. Mark the position of the screw holes to replace the feet as you go.
- Screw feet back in the base through the fabric.
- Turn under the ¾in (2cm) excess at the base of the pole and sew it to the knitted hexagon base with slipstitch.

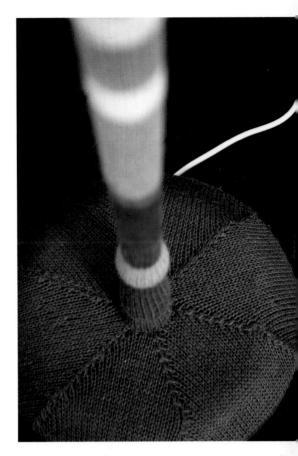

diamond cable bolster

A pattern inspired by traditional Aran knitting is given a fresh twist with a modern pillow shape. Cable patterns can look a bit complicated when written out, but this diamond repeat is easy enough once you settle into the rhythm of it.

Skill level ✳ ✳ ✳

Size
18in (45cm) long by 6¾in (17cm) diameter

Materials
YARN
Wool/alpaca yarn such as Creative Focus Worsted from Rowan—75% wool, 25% alpaca; approx. 220yds (200m) per 3½oz (100g) ball
- New Fern—approx. 7oz (200g)/ 440yds (400m)

NEEDLES
Pair of US 7 (4.5mm) knitting needles

OTHER MATERIALS
- Small cable needle
- Bolster pad measuring 18in (45cm) long by 6¾in (17cm) diameter
- Tapestry needle
- Three ¾in (2cm) buttons (I have chosen vintage horn ones)

Gauge (tension)
19 sts and 24 rows to 4in (10cm) over patt using US 7 (4.5mm) needles

Abbreviations
C4B—cable 4 back: slip next 2 sts onto cable needle and hold at back of work, knit next 2 sts from left-hand needle, then knit 2 sts from cable needle.
C3L—cable 3 left: slip next 2 sts onto cable needle and hold at front of work, purl next st from left-hand needle, then knit 2 sts from cable needle.
C3R—cable 3 right: slip next st onto cable needle and hold at back of work, knit next 2 sts from left-hand needle, then purl st from cable needle.
See also page 124

Pattern
MAIN PIECE
Cast on 86 sts.
Row 1: P2, [k2, p2] to end.
Row 2: K2, [p2, k2] to end.
Row 3 (buttonhole row): [P2, k2] 6 times, p2, yo, k2tog, [p2, k2] 3 times, p2, yo, k2tog, [p2, k2] 3 times, p2, k2tog, yo, p2, [k2, p2] 6 times.
Row 4: K2, [p2, k2] to end.
Rows 5–6: Work every st in 2x2 rib patt as it presents.
Row 7: K1, [k2, p8, k2] 7 times, k1.
Row 8 and every alt row: K1, work every st in patt as it presents to last st, k1.
Row 9: K3, p8, [C4B, p8] 6 times, k3.

Row 11: K1, [C3L, p6, C3R] 7 times, k1.

Row 13: K1, [p1, C3L, p4, C3R, p1] 7 times, k1.

Row 15: K1, [p2, C3L, p2, C3R, p2] 7 times, k1.

Row 17: K1, [p3, C3L, C3R, p3] 7 times, k1.

Row 19: K1, [p4, C4B, p4] 7 times, k1.

Row 21: K1, work every st in patt as it presents, k1.

Row 23: K1, [p4, C4B, p4] 7 times, k1.

Row 25: K1, [p3, C3R, C3L, p3] 7 times, k1.

Row 27: K1, [p2, C3R, p2, C3L, p2] 7 times, k1.

Row 29: K1, [p1, C3R, p4, C3L, p1] 7 times, k1.

Row 31: K1, [C3R, p6, C3L] 7 times, k1.

Row 33: K3, [p8, C4B] 6 times, p8, k2, k1.

Row 34: K1, work every st in patt as it presents, k1.

Rep rows 7–34, 4 more times.

Row 147: [P2, k2] to last 2 sts, p2.

Rows 148–152: Work every st in 2x2 rib patt as it presents.

Bind (cast) off.

BOLSTER END

(Make two)

Cast on 103 sts.

Row 1 (WS) and every alt row: Purl.

Row 2: K2tog, k14, [sk2po, k14] 5 times, skpo. *91 sts*

Row 3: K2tog, k12, [sk2po, k12] 5 times, skpo. *79 sts*

Row 4: K2tog, k10, [sk2po, k10] 5 times, skpo. *67 sts*

Row 5: K2tog, k8, [sk2po, k8] 5 times, skpo. *55 sts*

Row 6: K2tog, k6, [sk2po, k6] 5 times, skpo. *43 sts*

Row 7: K2tog, k4, [sk2po, k4] 5 times, skpo. *31 sts*

Row 9: K2tog, k2, [sk2po, k2] 5 times, skpo. *19 sts*

Row 11: K2tog, [sk2po] 5 times, skpo. *7 sts*

Break yarn, thread end through remaining sts and draw tight.

TO MAKE UP

• Weave in all loose ends. Press the knitting gently following the instructions on the yarn wrapper.

• Wrong side out, wrap the main piece around the pad, placing the buttonhole rib UNDER the plain rib. Pin the ends in place then sew them on with backstitch. Take the cover off the pad and turn right side out. Sew buttons on the plain rib to align with the buttonholes. Put the pad in the cover, the buttonhole rib should now be on top of the plain rib. Fasten the buttons, then using yarn, sew the rib in position for approx. 3in (8cm) at each end of the bolster.

Choosing a color
I've chosen to work in a favorite color, but this pattern would also look stunning in natural ecru to reflect the traditional knit pattern.

honeycomb pillow

This lovely pillow will add color and texture with subtle effect. The pattern looks complicated, but you only work with one color yarn at a time, so actually it's really quite easy to do.

Skill level ✳ ✳

Size

16 x 16in (40 x 40cm)

Materials

YARN

Wool/alpaca yarn such as Creative Focus Worsted from Rowan—75% wool, 25% alpaca; approx. 220yds (200m) per 3½oz (100g) ball

- Basil (A)—approx. 3½oz (100g)/ 220yds (200m)
- Teal (B)—approx. 1¾oz (50g)/ 110yds (100m)

NEEDLES

Pair of US 7 (4.5mm) knitting needles

OTHER MATERIALS

- 16 x 16in (40 x 40cm) pillow pad
- Fabric for back of pillow
- Pins
- Sewing needle
- Sewing thread

Gauge (tension)

19 sts and 35 rows to 4in (10cm) over patt using US 7 (4.5mm) needles

Abbreviations

sl2p wyb—slip 2 sts purlwise with yarn at back
sl2p wyf—slip 2 sts purlwise with yarn in front
See also page 124

Pattern
PILLOW FRONT
Using A, cast on 78 sts.

Row 1 (RS): Knit.

Row 2: Purl.

Change to B.

Row 3: Purl.

Row 4: Knit.

Change to A.

Row 5: K2, [sl2p wyb, k6] to last 4 sts, sl2p, k2.

Row 6: P2 [sl2p wyf, p6] to last 4 sts, sl2p, p2.

Rep rows 5–6 twice more.

Change to B.

Row 11: Purl.

Row 12: Knit.

Change to A.

Row 13: K6, [sl2p wyb, k6] to end.

Row 14: P6 [sl2p wyf, p6] to end.

Rep rows 13–14 twice more.

Rep rows 3–18, 8 more times, until work measures approx. 16¾in (42cm) from cast on edge.

Change to B.

Rep rows 3–4.

Change to A.

Rep rows 1–2.

Bind (cast) off.

TO MAKE UP
● Weave in all loose ends. Press the knitting gently following the instructions on the yarn wrapper.

● I chose dark brown canvas for the back of this pillow. Cut the fabric ⅜in (1cm) larger than the knitted panel to allow for fraying.

● Right sides together, pin the fabric to the knitted panel. Taking a ⅝in (1.5cm) seam allowance on the knitted panel, sew around three sides using a sewing machine or by hand using backstitch.

● Turn cover right side out and insert pillow pad. Hand-sew final side closed with slipstitch.

Make two
Create an exciting pair of pillows by swapping colors A and B for the second one.

CHARGED 2/- 1963

chunky cable pillow

This pillow is a great way to add texture into your home with a quick and easy knit project. I've used a soft color yarn, but the pattern looks great in a bright and bold color, too.

Skill level ✳ ✳

Size
18 x 18in (45 x 45cm)

Materials
YARN
- Wool yarn such as Big Wool from Rowan—100% merino wool; approx. 87yds (80m) per 3½oz (100g) ball
- Eternal—approx. 7oz (200g)/174yds (160m)

NEEDLES
Pair of US 15 (10mm) knitting needles

OTHER MATERIALS
- Large cable needle
- 18 x 18in (45 x 45cm) pillow pad
- Fabric for back of pillow
- Pins
- Sewing needle
- Sewing thread

Gauge (tension)
8 sts and 12 rows to 4in (10cm) over rev st st using US 15 (10mm) needles

Abbreviations
C8F—cable 8 forward: slip next 4 sts onto cable needle and hold at front of work, knit next 4 sts from left-hand needle, then knit 4 sts from cable needle. See also page 124

Pattern
PILLOW FRONT
Cast on 42 sts.
Row 1: K1, [p4, k8] 3 times, p4, k1.
Row 2: K1, [k4, p8] 3 times, k5.
Rows 3–6: Rep rows 1–2 twice more.
Row 7: K1, p4, k8, p4, C8F, p4, k8, p4, k1.
Rows 8–12: Rep rows 2–6 once more.
Row 13: K1, p4, C8F, p4, k8, p4, C8F, p4, k1.
Rep rows 2–13, 3 more times.
Rep rows 2–6 once.
Bind (cast) off.

TO MAKE UP
- Weave in all loose ends. Press the knitting gently, avoiding the cabled sections, following the instructions on the yarn wrapper.
- I chose a vintage fabric for the back of this pillow. Cut the fabric ⅜in (1cm) larger than the knitted panel to allow for fraying.
- Right sides together, pin the fabric to the knitted panel. Taking a ⅝in (1.5cm) seam allowance on the knitted panel, sew around three sides using a sewing machine, or by hand using backstitch.
- Turn cover right side out and insert pillow pad. Hand-sew final side closed with slipstitch.

Washing warning
This yarn says that it can be hand washed, but in order to keep the super chunky texture I have found that it is best not to wash it.

stripe pillow

An incredibly simple pillow to make, but bold colors make this a stylish project for the home. Choose a favorite palette, or colors to match a room scheme to personalize your pillow.

Skill level ✳

Size
16 x 16in (40 x 40cm)

Materials
YARN

Wool/alpaca yarn such as Creative Focus Worsted from Rowan—75% wool, 25% alpaca; approx. 220yds (200m) per 3½oz (100g) ball
- New Fern (A)—approx. 1¼oz (35g)/ 77yds (70m)
- Teal (B)—approx. 1¼oz (35g)/ 77yds (70m)
- Cobalt (C)—approx. 1oz (25g)/ 55yds (50m)
- Golden Heather (D)—approx. ¼oz (10g)/22yds (20m)
- Basil (E)—approx. 1oz (25g)/ 55yds (50m)

NOTE: Use two ends of yarn held together throughout.

NEEDLES
Pair of US 10 (6mm) knitting needles

OTHER MATERIALS
- 16 x 16in (40 x 40cm) pillow pad
- Fabric for back of pillow
- Pins
- Sewing needle
- Sewing thread

Gauge (tension)
12 sts and 18 rows to 4in (10cm) over st st using US 10 (6mm) needles

Abbreviations
See page 124

Pattern

PILLOW FRONT

Using A, cast on 52 sts.

Rows 1–14: Knit.

Change to B.

Row 15: [K1, p1] to end.

Row 16: [P1, k1] to end.

Rep rows 15–16 twice more.

Change to C.

Rep rows 1–14 once.

Change to D.

Rep rows 15–20 once.

Change to E.

Rep rows 1–12 once.

Change to A.

Rep rows 15–20 once.

Change to B.

Row 59: Knit.

Row 60: Purl

Rep rows 59–60, 10 more times.

Bind (cast) off.

TO MAKE UP

• Weave in all loose ends. Press the knitting gently, avoiding the cabled sections, following the instructions on the yarn wrapper.

• I chose a dark brown canvas fabric for the back of this pillow. Cut the fabric ⅜in (1cm) larger than the knitted panel to allow for fraying.

• Right sides together, pin the fabric to the knitted panel. Taking a ⅝in (1.5cm) seam allowance on the knitted panel, sew around three sides using a sewing machine, or by hand using backstitch.

• Turn cover right side out and insert pillow pad. Hand-sew final side closed with slipstitch.

Mix and match
This pillow and the honeycomb pillow (see page 51) contrast beautifully and make a lovely pair.

giant knit pouffe

Knit your own wonderfully retro pouffe. It can be used to put your feet up, or as an additional seat, so it's practical as well as good-looking.

Skill level ✳ ✳ ✳

Size
Approx. 12in (30cm) high by 56in (140cm) circumference

Materials
YARN
⅝in (15mm) thick black rope without core—approx. 88yds (80m)

NEEDLES
Pair of 1¾in (4.5cm) knitting needles

OTHER MATERIALS
- Black fabric to construct a beanbag (or cover a pillow pad)
- Beanbag beads (optional)
- Extra-large cable needle—I used a US 15 (10mm) knitting needle
- Sewing machine
- Sewing needle
- Sewing thread

Gauge (tension)
2.5 sts and 3 rows to 4in (10cm) over st st using 1¾in (4.5cm) needles

Abbreviations
C4B—cable 4 back: slip next 2 sts onto cable needle and hold at back of work, knit next 2 sts from left-hand needle, then knit 2 sts from cable needle.
Turn—turn the knitting as though you have completed the row. See also page 124

Pattern
MAIN PIECE
Cast on 14 sts.

Row 1: P5, k4, p5.
Row 2: K5, p4, k1, turn.
Row 3: P1, C4B, p3, turn.
Row 4: K3, p4, k3, turn.
Row 5: P3, k4, p1, turn.
Row 6: K1, p4, k5.
Row 7: P5, k4, p5.
Row 8: K5, p4, k1, turn.
Row 9: P1, k4, p3, turn.
Row 10: K3, p4, k3, turn.
Row 11: P3, k4, p1, turn.
Row 12: K1, p4, k5.
Row 13: P5, C4B, p5.
Row 14: K5, p4, k1, turn.
Row 15: P1, k4, p3, turn.
Row 16: K3, p4, k3, turn.
Row 17: P3, k4, p1, turn.
Row 18: K1, p4, k5.
Row 19: P5, k4, p5.
Row 20: K5, p4, k1, turn.
Row 21: P1, k4, p3, turn.
Row 22: K3, p4, k3, turn.
Row 23: P3, C4B, p1, turn.
Row 24: K1, p4, k5.
Rows 25–30: As rows 7–12.
Rows 31–42: As rows 1–12.
Bind (cast) off.

TO MAKE UP
● Construct the drum-shaped inner pad of the pouffe by cutting black fabric into two circles with diameter of 20½in (52cm) and a length measuring 61in (155cm) by depth 8in (20cm). Taking a ³⁄₈in (1cm) seam allowance throughout, sew the short ends of the long strip together to form a tube. Right sides together, sew the fabric circles to the top and bottom of the tube, leaving a 4in (10cm) gap in one seam for filling. Turn right side out through the gap and fill with beanbag beads until firm. Sew the gap closed. Alternatively, buy a 22in (55cm) feather pillow pad to create a softer pouffe; cover the feather pad with black fabric.

● Insert the pad into the knitted cover through the open side seam (the cast on and bound (cast) off edges form the side seam.) Lace the side seam closed with rope. Bind the ends of the rope with matching sewing thread and sew them down unobtrusively. Using the remaining rope, gather the top and bottom tightly to close the knitting into a ball.

Filling the pouffe
If you make your pouffe in a different-colored rope, then match the pad fabric to the rope color to stop the pad showing through the knitting.

large floor pillow

A wonderfully textured floor pillow, which has been felted for a hardwearing finish. This is a very simple stitch pattern to work and the chunky yarn and big needles mean that the knitting will "grow" quickly.

Skill level ✳

Size
25½ x 25½in (65 x 65cm)

Materials
YARN
A lightly twisted wool, also known as a pencil roving, such as Bella from Texere—100% pure wool; approx. 142yds (130m) per 7oz (200g) ball
- Ecru—approx. 14oz (400g)/184yds (160m)

NEEDLES
Pair of US 19 (15mm) knitting needles

OTHER MATERIALS
- 25½ x 25½in (65 x 65cm) pillow pad
- Fabric for pillow back
- Pins
- Sewing needle
- Sewing thread

Gauge (tension)
8 sts and 10 rows to 4in (10cm) over patt using US 19 (15mm) needles

Abbreviations
See page 124

Pattern
PILLOW FRONT
Cast on 64 sts.
Row 1: [Yo, k2, pass yo over the k2] to end.
Row 2: Purl.
Row 3: K1, [yo, k2, pass yo over the k2] to last st, k1.
Row 4: Purl.
Rep rows 1–4 until knitting measures 27½in (70cm).
Bind (cast) off.

TO MAKE UP
- Weave in all loose ends. Wash the knit gently by hand until it is felted to the desired degree (see page 121). Leave to dry.
- As the pillow is intended to sit on the floor, I chose a hardwearing canvas fabric for the back. Cut the fabric ⅜in (1cm) larger than the knitted panel to allow for fraying.
- Right sides together, pin the fabric to the knitted panel. Taking a ⅝in (1.5cm) seam allowance on the knitted panel, sew around three sides using a sewing machine, or by hand using backstitch.
- Turn cover right side out and insert pillow pad. Hand-sew final side closed with slipstitch.

Functional felting
This yarn will felt very easily, so by washing it by hand you can really control the desired result.

cable trim wastebasket

Get rid of an ugly but necessary piece of household furniture and substitute a desirable knitted version by working a cover for a standard metal wastebasket.

Skill level ✳ ✳ ✳

Size
10¼in (26cm) high by 10in (25cm) square on the top edge

Materials
YARN
Wool yarn such as Pure Wool DK from Rowan—100% wool; approx. 137 yds (125m) per 1¾oz (50g) ball
- Anthracite—approx. 7oz (200g)/548yds (500m)

NEEDLES
Pair of US 10 (6mm) knitting needles

OTHER MATERIALS
- Square wastebasket measuring 10¼in (26cm) high by 10in (25cm) square on the top edge and 6in (15cm) square on the bottom edge
- Large cable needle
- Glue gun

Gauge (tension)
13 sts and 20 rows to 4in (10cm) over rev st st using US 10 (6mm) needles

Abbreviations
C8F—cable 8 forward: slip next 4 sts onto cable needle and hold at front of work, knit next 4 sts from left-hand needle, then knit 4 sts from cable needle. See also page 124

Pattern

BASE

Cast on 22 sts.

Row 1 (RS): Purl.

Row 2: Knit.

These 2 rows form rev st st.

Work 30 more rows rev st st.

This square forms the base of the wastebasket cover.

FIRST SIDE

Row 33: Bind (cast) off 4 sts, p to end. *18 sts*

***Row 34:** Cast on 4 sts, p8, k to end. *22 sts*

Rows 35–38: Work every st in patt as it presents.

Row 39: P1, m1, p13, m1, C8F. *24 sts*

Rows 40–44: Work every st in patt as it presents.

Row 45: P1, m1, p15, m1, k8. *26 sts*

Rows 46–50: Work every st in patt as it presents.

Row 51: P1, m1, p17, m1, C8F. *28 sts*

Rows 52–56: Work every st in patt as it presents.

Row 57: P1, m1, p19, m1, k8. *30 sts*

Rows 58–62: Work every st in patt as it presents.

Row 63: P1, m1, p21, m1, C8F. *32 sts*

Rows 64–68: Work every st in patt as it presents.

Row 69: P1, m1, p23, m1, k8. *34 sts*

Rows 70–74: Work every st in patt as it presents.

Row 75: P1, m1, p25, m1, C8F. *36 sts*

Rows 76–80: Work every st in patt as it presents.

Row 81: [K2, p2] to end.

Rows 82–83: Work every st in patt as it presents.

Bind (cast) off. *

Rows 34–83 have created the first side section of the cover.

SECOND SIDE

**Lay knitting flat with RS facing and side section just worked to the right. Beg 1¼in (3cm) along from RH end of top edge of base square (edge that is to the left of first side section), pick up 18 sts along this edge.

Rep from * to * to complete the second side section of the cover.**

THIRD AND FOURTH SIDES

Rep from ** to ** twice more to complete all four knitted side sections.

TO MAKE UP

● Weave in all loose ends. Press the knitting gently, avoiding the cables, following the instructions on the yarn wrapper.

● Wrap the knitting over the metal wastebasket and sew the side seams using mattress stitch. Each cable should be on a corner of the basket and the seams should be ¾in (2cm) along the side panels. Sew the cables to the base to form base points. Fold the top edge of the knitting over the top edge of the wastebasket, pulling the knitting tight, and secure it with glue.

Covering up

When securing the knitted cover inside the top edge it is important that the knitting is pulled tight so that it doesn't bag out on the sides of the wastebasket.

CHAPTER 3

pale
palette

Natural colors are
complemented with soft
shades in a collection
that's perfectly suited to
modern minimal living.

cable lampshade

Chunky cables accentuate the curve of this textured lampshade. Use it as a pendant shade, or it looks equally chic on a natural-colored version of the knitted lampstand on page 44.

Skill level ✳ ✳ ✳

Size

10in (25cm) high with bottom diameter of 16in (40cm)

Materials

YARN

Wool/alpaca yarn such as Creative Focus Worsted from Rowan—75% wool, 25% alpaca; approx. 220yds (200m) per 3½oz (100g) ball

- Natural—approx. 10½oz (300g)/ 660yds (600m)

NOTE: Use two ends of yarn held together throughout

NEEDLES

Pair of US 10 (6mm) knitting needles

OTHER MATERIALS

- Large cable needle
- 10in (25cm) high flared lampshade with bottom diameter of 16in (40cm) (see Resources, page 126)
- Tapestry needle
- Elastic cord in color to match yarn

Gauge (tension)

10 sts and 15 rows to 4in (10cm) over st st using US 10 (6mm) needles

Abbreviations

C6F—cable 6 forward: slip next 3 sts onto cable needle and hold at front of work, knit next 3 sts from left-hand needle, then knit 3 sts from cable needle. C8F—cable 8 forward: slip next 4 sts onto cable needle and hold at front of work, knit next 4 sts from left-hand needle, then knit 4 sts from cable needle. C10F—cable 10 forward: slip next 5 sts onto cable needle and hold at front of work, knit next 5 sts from left-hand needle, then knit 5 sts from cable needle. Turn—turn the knitting as though you have completed the row. See also page 124

Pattern
MAIN PIECE
Cast on 38 sts.

Row 1: P3, k6, p4, k8, p4, k10, p3.

Row 2: K3, p10, k4, p8, k4, p6, k3.

Rep rows 1–2 once more.

Row 5: P3, C6F, p4, k8, p4, k10, p3.

Row 6: K3, p10, k4, p8, k4, p6, k3.

Row 7: P3, k6, p4, k8, p4, k10, p3.

Row 8: K3, p10, k4, p8, k2, turn.

Cont on 27 sts, 11 sts rem on LH needle.

Row 9: P2, C8F, p4, k10, p3.

Row 10: K3, p10, k2, turn.

Cont on 15 sts, 23 sts rem on LH needle.

Row 11: P2, C10F, p3.

Row 12: K3, p10, k4, p8, k4, p6, k3.

Row 13: P3, k6, p4, k8, p4, k10, p3.

Row 14: K3, p10, k4, p8, k2, turn.

Cont on 27 sts, 11 sts rem on LH needle.

Row 15: P2, k8, p4, k10, p3.

Row 16: K3, p10, k2, turn.

Cont on 15 sts, 23 sts rem on LH needle.

Row 17: P2, k10, p3.

Row 18: K3, p10, k4, p8, k4, p6, k3.

Rep rows 5–18, 14 more times.

Bind (cast) off.

TO MAKE UP
- Weave in all loose ends. Press the knitting gently, avoiding the cable sections, following the instructions on the yarn wrapper.
- Using mattress stitch, sew together the cast on and bound (cast) off ends to form a knitted tube. Using the tapestry needle, thread elastic through the knitting around the top and bottom of the knitted cover. Slip the cover over the shade and pull the elastic tight so that the cover perfectly fits the shade. Knot the ends of the elastic and trim them short.

Covering a shade
If you have an existing lampshade, this pattern will create a cover that will fit over a lampshade up to 12in (30cm) in diameter.

table runner

Inspired by traditional woven table runners, this pattern should be knitted with very loose gauge. You might find this awkward at first, so practice with some scrap yarn before starting the runner.

Skill level ✳ ✳

Size
Approx. 69½ x 10in (176 x 25cm)

Materials

YARN

Cotton yarn such as Cotton Glace from Rowan—100% cotton; approx. 125 yds (115m) per 1¾oz (50g) ball
- Dawn Grey—approx. 7oz (200g)/ 500yds (460m)

NEEDLES

Pair of US 10 (6mm) knitting needles

OTHER MATERIALS
- Medium cable needle
- Tapestry needle

Gauge (tension)
18 sts and 19 rows to 4in (10cm) over rev st st using US 10 (6mm) needles

Abbreviations
C4F—cable 4 forward: slip next 2 sts onto cable needle and hold at front of work, knit next 2 sts from left-hand needle, then knit 2 sts from cable needle.
C3L—cable 3 left: slip next 2 sts onto cable needle and hold at front of work, purl next st from left-hand needle, then knit 2 sts from cable needle.
C3R—cable 3 right: slip next st onto cable needle and hold at back of work, knit next 2 sts from left-hand needle, then purl st from cable needle.
See also page 124

Pattern

MAIN PIECE

Cast on 50 sts.

Row 1: K2 [p2, k2] to end.

Rows 2–24: Work every st in 2x2 rib patt as it presents.

Row 25: K2, p2, k2, p17, k4, p17, k2, p2, k2.

Row 26 and every alt row: Work every st in patt as it presents.

Row 27: K2, p2, k2, p17, C4F, p17, k2, p2, k2.

Row 29: K2, p2, k2, p16, C3R, C3L, p16, k2, p2, k2.

Row 31: K2, p2, k2, p15, C3R, p2, C3L, p15, k2, p2, k2.

Row 33: K2, p2, k2, p14, C3R, p4, C3L, p14, k2, p2, k2.

Row 35: K2, p2, k2, p13, C3R, p6, C3L, p13, k2, p2, k2.

Row 37: K2, p2, k2, p12, C3R, p8, C3L, p12, k2, p2, k2.

Row 39: Work every st in patt as it presents.

Row 41: K2, p2, k2, p12, C3L, p8, C3R, p12, k2, p2, k2.

Row 43: K2, p2, k2, p13, C3L, p6, C3R, p13, k2, p2, k2.

Row 45: K2, p2, k2, p14, C3L, p4, C3R, p14, k2, p2, k2.

Row 47: K2, p2, k2, p15, C3L, p2, C3R, p15, k2, p2, k2.

Row 49: K2, p2, k2, p16, C3L, C3R, p16, k2, p2, k2.

Row 51: K2, p2, k2, p17, C4F, p17, k2, p2, k2.

Row 53: Work every st in patt as it presents.

Row 54: As row 26.

Rep rows 27–54, 9 more times.

Rep rows 1–24 once more.

Bind (cast) off.

TO MAKE UP

● Weave in all loose ends. Wash the knit gently by hand and leave to dry flat.

smoothing stitches
Loose gauge knitting can be very unforgiving, but washing the table runner will help even out the stitches.

honeycomb footstool

Revamp your own vintage stool with a bespoke cover that can be worked to fit different-sized stools. Make yours in two colors that suit your room scheme.

Skill level ✳ ✳

Size

Can be adjusted to fit your own stool (see page 123)

Materials

YARN

Cotton yarn such as Cotton Glace from Rowan—100% cotton; approx. 125yds (115m) per 1¾oz (50g) ball
- Dawn Grey (A)—approx. 10½oz (300g)/375yds (345m)

Wool yarn such as Pure Wool DK from Rowan—100% wool; approx. 137yds (125m) per 1¾oz (50g) ball
- Pure Wool DK in Anthracite (B)— approx. 3½oz (100g)/274yds (250m)

NOTE: Use two ends of yarn held together throughout

NEEDLES

Pair of US 10 (6mm) knitting needles

OTHER MATERIALS
- Vintage stool with upholstery intact
- Tapestry needle
- Staple gun
- Black fabric to cover underside of stool

Gauge (tension)

18 sts and 23 rows to 4in (10cm) over patt using US 10 (6mm) needles

Abbreviations

sl2p wyb—slip 2 sts purlwise with yarn at back
sl2p wyf—slip 2 sts purlwise with yarn in front
See also page 124

Pattern

MAIN PIECE

Using A, cast on required number of sts (multiple of 8 + 6 sts).
Row 1 (RS): Knit.
Row 2: Purl.
Change to B.
Row 3: Purl.
Row 4: Knit.
Change to A.
Row 5: K2, [sl2p wyb, k6] to last 4 sts, sl2p, k2.

Row 6: P2 [sl2p wyf, p6] to last 4 sts, sl2p, p2.
Rep rows 5–6 twice more.
Change to B.
Row 11: Purl.
Row 12: Knit.
Change to A.
Row 13: K2, [sl2p wyb, k6] to last 4 sts, sl2p, k2.
Row 14: P2 [sl2p wyf, p6] to last 4 sts, sl2p, p2.
Rep rows 13–14 twice more.
Rep rows 3–18 until work is long enough to completely cover the stool pad with extra to secure underneath.
Bind (cast) off.

TO MAKE UP
- Weave in all loose ends.
- Stretch the knitting over the stool pad and secure it underneath with the staple gun. Start in the middle of one side and work out, then fold the corners of the knitting neatly and staple them in place. Then fasten the opposite side, then the remaining sides.
- Cover the underneath of the seat with black fabric, turning under the edges of the fabric and overlapping the edges of the knitting, then staple the fabric in place.

cable vase cuff

Chic and understated, this cuff will add style to a simple vase. Make a number of them in different colors then you can dress your vase to match your flowers.

Skill level ✳ ✳

Size

4¾in (12cm) wide by 7in (18cm) in diameter

Materials

YARN

Double knitting yarn such as Baby Bamboo from Sirdar—80% bamboo, 20% wool; approx. 104yds (95m) in a 1¾oz (50g) ball

- Putty—approx. 1¾oz (50g)/ 104yds (95m)

NEEDLES

Pair of US 6 (4mm) knitting needles

OTHER MATERIALS

- Medium cable needle
- Glass vase measuring 7in (18cm) in diameter (see Resources, page 126)

Gauge (tension)

30 sts and 28 rows to 4in (10cm) over cable patt using US 6 (4mm) needles

Abbreviations

C4F—cable 4 back: slip next 2 sts onto cable needle and hold at back of work, knit next 2 sts from left-hand needle, then knit 2 sts from cable needle.
C3L—cable 3 left: slip next 2 sts onto cable needle and hold at front of work, purl next st from left-hand needle, then knit 2 sts from cable needle.
C3R—cable 3 right: slip next st onto cable needle and hold at back of work, knit next 2 sts from left-hand needle, then purl st from cable needle.
See also page 124

Pattern
CABLE SECTION
Cast on 26 sts.

Row 1: K1, [k2, p8, k2] twice, k1.

Row 2 and every alt row: Work every st in patt as it presents.

Row 3: K1, k2, p8, C4B, p8, k2, k1.

Row 5: K1, [C3L, p6, C3R] twice, k1.

Row 7: K1, [p1, C3L, p4, C3R, p1] twice, k1.

Row 9: K1, [p2, C3L, p2, C3R, p2] twice, k1.

Row 11: K1, [p3, C3L, C3R, p3] twice, k1.

Row 13: K1, [p4, C4B, p4] twice, k1.

Row 15: K1, work every st in patt as it presents, k1.

Row 17: K1, [p4, C4B, p4] twice, k1.

Row 19: K1, [p3, C3R, C3L, p3] twice, k1.

Row 21: K1, [p2, C3R, p2, C3L, p2] twice, k1.

Row 23: K1, [p1, C3R, p4, C3L, p1] twice, k1.

Row 25: K1, [C3R, p6, C3L] twice, k1.

Row 27: K1, k2, p8, C4B, p8, k2, k1.

Row 28: As row 2.

Rep rows 1–28, 4 more times.

Bind (cast) off.

RIB TRIM
Pick up 90 sts along right side edge.

Row 1: [K2, p2] to last 2 sts, k2.

Rows 2–4: Knit each st as it presents.

Bind (cast) off.

Rep along left side edge.

TO MAKE UP
- Weave in all loose ends. Press the knitting gently following the instructions on the yarn wrapper.
- Using mattress stitch (see page 114), sew the cast on edge to the bound (cast) off edge to form a knitted tube.
- Slip the cuff over the vase.

Picking up stitches
If you've not picked up stitches in knitting before, turn to page 113 for instructions on how to do this: it's not difficult!

knitted cable rug

This soft and luscious rug is all about the yarn.
It will take as long to prepare the roving for knitting
as it will to actually knit the rug on giant needles,
but it is worth it!

Skill level ✳ ✳ ✳

Size

Approx. 53 x 31½in (135 x 80cm)

Materials

YARN

Wool roving such as Wool Tops 64's
Ecru from Texere—soft, fine merino wool;
14oz (400g) bag
- Ecru—approx. 3lb 8oz (1.6kg)

NEEDLES

Pair of 1¾in (4.5cm) knitting needles
(see Resources, page 126)

OTHER MATERIALS

- Extra-large cable needle (I used a
  US 15/10mm knitting needle)
- Two large double bed sheets
- Liquid washing detergent
- String
- Bathtub
- Clean rubber boots
- Drying rack

Gauge (tension)

3 sts and 4.5 rows to 4in (10cm) over
rev st st using 1¾in (4.5cm) needles

Abbreviations

C4F—cable 4 forward: slip next 2 sts
onto cable needle and hold at front of
work, knit next 2 sts from left-hand
needle, then knit 2 sts from cable needle.
C3L—cable 3 left: slip next 2 sts onto
cable needle and hold at front of work,
purl next st from left-hand needle, then
knit 2 sts from cable needle.
C3R—cable 3 right: slip next st onto
cable needle and hold at back of work,
knit next 2 sts from left-hand needle, then
purl st from cable needle.
See also page 124

To prepare the yarn

- Preparing the roving for knitting is very
important as it is necessary to make it
strong enough. You do not want to fully
felt the fibers, but the roving should feel
firmer, and as though it has puffed up
slightly.
- Place a double sheet flat on the floor
and, starting in one corner and pulling
the roving out of the bag as you go, lay
a continuous length of roving along one
side, following the edge of the sheet.
When you reach the opposite corner,
don't break off the roving but fold the

sheet over to fully cover the wool, then
lay another line of roving parallel to the
previous length. Continue in this way until
you have fully laid out and wrapped as
much roving as will fit on the sheet,
ensuring that the sheet fabric is always
separating the lengths of roving so that
they will not felt together. Tie a length of
string every 8in (20cm) down the bundle
to hold it closed. Start a new sheet and
wrap more roving in the same way. You
will probably need to make four of these
bundles in total, but I have found that the
felting works best with two at a time.
- Fill the bathtub with the hottest tap
water possible and put in as much
washing detergent as for a normal single
load in your washing machine. Lay the
bundles in the hot water. Wearing the
rubber boots, climb into the bath and
stomp on the bundles for about five
minutes to encourage a certain amount of
felting. Drain the bath, then rinse the
bundles several times with cold water to
remove any trace of detergent.
- Spin the bundles dry if you have a
washing machine, or squeeze them until
you have removed as much water as
possible if you do not. Open the bundles

and lay the now slightly felted wool on a drying rack for at least 12 hours to dry. Repeat until you have felted all four bags of roving.

• Once the wool is fully dry, pull the end of one length apart so that the roving is split evenly into two: as you gently pull, the roving should easily split down the entire length. Repeat this on each split length so that the original length is now split into four. Ball up your newly created yarn.

Pattern
MAIN PIECE

Cast on 24 sts.

Row 1: K1, p9, k4, p9, k1.
Row 2: K1, p1, k8, p4, k8, p1, k1.
Row 3: K1, p1, p8, k4, p8, p1, k1.
Row 4: K1, p1, k8, p4, k8, p1, k1.
Row 5: K1, p1, p8, C4F, p8, p1, k1.
Row 6: K1, p1, k8, p4, k8, p1, k1.
Row 7: K1, p1, p7, C3R, C3L, p7, p1, k1.
Row 8: K1, p1, k7, p2, k1, p1, p2, k7, p1, k1.
Row 9: K1, p1, p6, C3R, p1, k1, C3L, p6, p1, k1.
Row 10: K1, p1, k6, p2, [p1, k1] twice, p2, k6, p1, k1.
Row 11: K1, p1, p5, C3R, [k1, p1] twice, C3L, p5, p1, k1.
Row 12: K1, p1, k5, p2, [k1, p1] 3 times, p2, k5, p1, k1.
Row 13: K1, p1, p4, C3R, [p1, k1] 3 times, C3L, p4, p1, k1.
Row 14: K1, p1, k4, p2, [p1, k1] 4 times, p2, k4, p1, k1.
Row 15: K1, p1, p3, C3R, [k1, p1] 4 times, C3L, p3, p1, k1.
Row 16: K1, p1, k3, p2, [k1, p1] 5 times, p2, k3, p1, k1.
Row 17: K1, p1, p3, k2, [p1, k1] 5 times, k2, p3, p1, k1.
Row 18: K1, p1, k3, p2, [k1, p1] 5 times, p2, k3, p1, k1.
Row 19: K1, p1, p4, C3L, [p1, k1] 3 times, C3R, p4, p1, k1.
Row 20: K1, p1, k5, p2, [k1, p1] 3 times, p2, k5, p1, k1.
Row 21: K1, p1, p5, C3L, [k1, p1] twice, C3R, p5, p1, k1.
Row 22: K1, p1, k6, p2, [p1, k1] twice, p2, k6, p1, k1.
Row 23: K1, p1, p6, C3L, p1, k1, C3R, p6, p1, k1.
Row 24: K1, p1, k7, p2, k1, p1, p2, k7, p1, k1.
Row 25: K1, p1, p7, C3L, C3R, p7, p1, k1.
Row 26: K1, p1, k8, p4, k8, p1, k1.
Row 27: K1, p1, p8, C4F, p8, p1, k1.
Row 28: K1, p1, k8, p4, k8, p1, k1.
Row 29: K1, p1, p8, C4F, p8, p1, k1.
Row 30: K1, p1, k8, p4, k8, p1, k1.
Rep rows 3–30 once more, then row 3 once more.
Bind (cast) off knitwise on WS.

TO MAKE UP

• Weave in all loose ends.

splitting the yarn
Try to split the roving as evenly as possible, but don't worry if it is not all exactly the same—this will just add to the lovely texture.

knitted wall hearts

Cute and cozy textured wall art. Each box makes a pair of love hearts and you can cover them in the same color or in different shades or colors to create customized pieces for your home.

Skill level ✳ ✳

Size
9½in (24cm) high by 10¼in (26cm) wide

Materials
YARN
Wool yarn such as Big Wool from Rowan—100% merino wool; approx. 87yds (80m) per 3½oz (100g) ball
- Large heart—approx. 2¼oz (60g)/52yds (48m)
- Small heart—approx. 1½oz (40g)/35yds (32m)

NEEDLES
Pair of US 17 (12mm) knitting needles

OTHER MATERIALS
- Box (see Resources, page 126)
- Polyester stuffing
- Piece of fabric cut to shape 2½in (6cm) larger than the box, or 1½in (4cm) larger than the lid (I used a fine knit jersey)
- Piece of fabric cut the same size as the box or lid plus ¾in (2cm) hem allowance, to cover the back
- 2¾in (7cm) length of string knotted into a 1¼in (3cm) loop
- Sewing needle
- Sewing thread
- Staple gun
- Tapestry needle

Gauge (tension)
7 sts and 10 rows to 4in (10cm) over st st using US 17 (12mm) needles

Abbreviations
Turn—turn the knitting as though you have completed the row.
See also page 124

Pattern

FOR BOTH PARTS

Cast on 2 sts.
Row 1: K1, m1, k1. *3 sts*
Row 2 and every alt row: Purl.
Row 3: K1, m1, k1, m1, k1. *5 sts*
Row 5: K2, m1, k1, m1, k2. *7 sts*
Row 7: K3, m1, k1, m1, k3. *9 sts*
Row 9: K4, m1, k1, m1, k4. *11 sts*
Row 11: K5, m1, k1, m1, k5. *13 sts*
Row 13: K6, m1, k1, m1, k6. *15 sts*
Row 15: K7, m1, k1, m1, k7. *17 sts*
Row 17: K8, m1, k1, m1, k8. *19 sts*
Row 19: K9, m1, k1, m1, k9. *21 sts*
Row 21: K10, m1, k1, m1, k10. *23 sts*
Row 23: K11, m1, k1, m1, k11. *25 sts*
Row 25: K12, m1, k1, m1, k12. *27 sts*
Row 27: K13, m1, k1, m1, k13. *29 sts*
Row 28: Purl.

FOR SHALLOW LID

Row 29: K14, k1 in back loop of st below next st then k1 in next st, k14. *30 sts*
Row 30: Purl.
Row 31: Ssk, k11, k2tog, turn.
Cont on these 13 sts and leave rem 15 sts on needle.
Row 33: Ssk, k9, k2tog. *11 sts*
Row 35: Ssk, k7, k2tog. *9 sts*
Row 37: Ssk, k5, k2tog. *7 sts*
Row 39: Ssk, k3, k2tog. *5 sts*
Row 41: Ssk, k1, k2tog. *3 sts*
Row 42: P3tog and fasten off.
With RS facing, rejoin yarn to rem 15 sts.
Next row: Ssk, k11, k2tog. *13 sts*
Next and every alt row: Purl.
Next row: Ssk, k9, k2tog. *11 sts*
Next row: Ssk, k7, k2tog. *9 sts*
Next row: Ssk, k5, k2tog. *7 sts*
Next row: Ssk, k3, k2tog. *5 sts*
Next row: Ssk, k1, k2tog. *3 sts*
Next row: P3tog and fasten off.

FOR DEEP BOX

Row 29: K14, m1, k1, m1, k14. *31 sts*
Row 31: K15, m1, k1, m1, k15. *33 sts*
Row 33: K16, k1 in back loop of st below next st then k1 in next st, k16. *34 sts*
Row 35: Ssk, k13, k2tog, turn.
Cont on these 15 sts and leave rem 17 sts on needle.
Row 37: Ssk, k11, k2tog. *13 sts*
Row 39: Ssk, k9, k2tog. *11 sts*
Row 41: Ssk, k7, k2tog. *9 sts*
Row 43: Ssk, k5, k2tog. *7 sts*
Row 45: Ssk, k3, k2tog. *5 sts*
Row 47: Ssk, k1, k2tog. *3 sts*
Row 48: P3tog and fasten off.
With RS facing, rejoin yarn to rem 17 sts.
Next row: Ssk, k13, k2tog. *15 sts*
Next and every alt row: Purl.
Next row: Ssk, k11, k2tog. *13 sts*
Next row: Ssk, k9, k2tog. *11 sts*
Next row: Ssk, k7, k2tog. *9 sts*
Next row: Ssk, k5, k2tog. *7 sts*
Next row: Ssk, k3, k2tog. *5 sts*
Next row: Ssk, k1, k2tog. *3 sts*
Next row: P3tog and fasten off.

TO MAKE UP

- The following instructions tell you how to cover the box or the lid.
- Weave in all loose ends. Press the knitting gently following the instructions on the yarn wrapper.
- Pierce a hole in the back of the box. Pass the string loop through the hole to the back and secure inside with a large knot. Fill the box with polyester stuffing.
- Stretch the appropriate larger piece of fabric over the box and secure on the back with staples. Stretch the knitting over the box and secure it in the same way.
- Cover the stapled back with the remaining piece of fabric, turning under the edges, and sew it to the knitting (remembering to pass the string loop through the fabric so that you can hang the heart).

Making up
Pick either a neutral color fabric or a color to tone with the yarn, as the fabric will show through the knitting.

chunky bramble throw

A sumptuous textured throw that you'll love to snuggle up in on the sofa, or keep in the bedroom as a shoulder wrap on chilly mornings.

Skill level ✳ ✳

Size
Approx. 39¾in (102cm) x 34½in (88cm)

Materials
YARN
Wool yarn such as Big Wool from Rowan—100% merino wool; approx. 87yds (80m) per 3½oz (100g) ball
- Eternal—approx. 1lb 5oz (600g)/522yds (480m)

NEEDLES
Pair of US 19 (15mm) knitting needles

OTHER MATERIALS
- Tapestry needle

Gauge (tension)
7.5 sts and 9 rows to 4in (10cm) over patt using US 19 (15mm) needles

Abbreviations
See page 124

Pattern
MAIN PIECE
Cast on 66 sts.
Row 1 and every alt row: Purl.
Row 2: K1, *p3tog, (k1, p1, k1) into next st*; rep from * to * to last st, k1.
Row 4: K1, *(k1, p1, k1) into next st, p3tog*; rep from * to * to last st, k1.
Rep rows 1–4 until just enough yarn remains to bind (cast) off.
Bind (cast) off.

TO MAKE UP
- Weave in all loose ends. Press the knitting gently following the instructions on the yarn wrapper.

Changing size
To increase the size of your throw, cast on extra stitches in multiples of 4.

curtain tie

Keep your curtains under control with quirky knitted curtain ties. Make yours to match your curtains, remembering that they don't have to be the same color to be a perfect pairing.

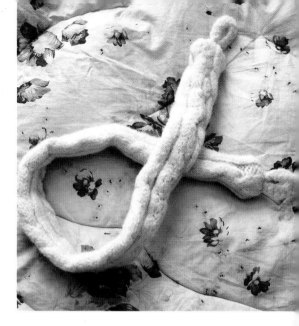

Skill level ✳ ✳ ✳

Size
Approx. 31½in (80cm) long by 4¾in (12cm) circumference

Materials
YARN
Wool yarn such as Chunky Wool from Texere—100% pure wool; approx. 120yds (110m) per 3½oz (100g) ball
- Ecru—4½oz (130g)/156yds (143m)

NEEDLES
Set of US 10 (6mm) double-pointed needles

OTHER MATERIALS
- Large cable needle
- J/10 (6mm) crochet hook

Gauge (tension)
12 sts and 17 rows to 4in (10cm) over patt using US 10 (6mm) needles

Abbreviations
C4F—cable 4 forward: slip next 2 sts onto cable needle and hold at front of work, knit next 2 sts from left-hand needle, then knit 2 sts from cable needle. See also page 124

Pattern
MAIN PIECE
Cast on 20 sts.
Evenly distribute the sts over 3 double-pointed needles.
Rounds 1–4: K2, p2, k4, p2, k2, p2, k4, p2.
Round 5: K2, p2, C4F, p2, k2, p2, k4, p2.
Rounds 6–8: K2, p2, k4, p2, k2, p2, k4, p2.
Round 9: K2, p2, k4, p2, k2, p2, C4F, p2.
Rep rounds 1–9, 22 more times.
Bind (cast) off.

LOOPS (MAKE TWO)
(Note that these are US crochet terms: turn to page 116 for UK equivalents.)
Row 1: Ch14.
Row 2: Work 1sc into each ch. Fasten off.

TO MAKE UP
- Weave in all loose ends. Sew one of the crochet loops to each end of the main piece.
- Wash the knit vigorously by hand until it is felted to the desired degree (see page 121). Leave to dry.

Functional felting
It is important to slightly felt the knitting in order to stop the curtain ties from stretching when you use them.

cable clock

An ever-popular clock from my collection; this version has a wonderful textured face knitted with rows of cables interspersed with narrow bands of stockinette.

Skill level ✳ ✳ ✳

Size
10in (25cm) diameter

Materials
YARN
Double knitting yarn such as Baby Bamboo from Sirdar—80% bamboo, 20% wool; approx. 104yds (95m) per 1¾oz (50g) ball
- Putty—approx. 3½oz (100g)/ 208yds (190m)

NOTE: Use two ends of yarn held together throughout

NEEDLES
Pair of US 9 (5.5mm) knitting needles

OTHER MATERIALS
- Medium cable needle
- 10in (25cm) diameter cardboard cake board
- Craft knife
- 11 x 11in (28 x 28cm) of thin foam
- Scissors
- Craft glue
- Quartz clock mechanism (see Resources, page 126)
- 10 x 10in (25 x 25cm) of fabric for the back
- String
- Tapestry needle
- Sewing needle
- Sewing thread

Gauge (tension)
15 sts and 19 rows to 4in (10cm) over patt using US 9 (5.5mm) needles

Abbreviations
C4F—cable 4 forward: slip next 2 sts onto cable needle and hold at front of work, knit next 2 sts from left-hand needle, then knit 2 sts from cable needle. C6F—cable 6 forward: slip next 3 sts onto cable needle and hold at front of work, knit next 3 sts from left-hand needle, then knit 3 sts from cable needle. See also page 124

Sweet Rose
Loves
Emblem
fond and true
Brings Greetings
for
this day
to you.
A Happy Birthday
POST CARD
BEST IN THE WORLD
To Janey
from Madge
A Happy
Easter.

Pattern
MAIN PIECE
Cast on 28 sts.

Row 1: P1, k4, p2, k2, p2, k6, p2, k2, p2, k4, p1.

Row 2 and every alt row: Work every st in patt as it presents.

Row 3: Inc, work every st in patt as it presents to last st, inc. *30 sts*

Row 5: Inc, work every st in patt as it presents to last st, inc. *32 sts*

Row 7: Inc, work every st in patt as it presents to last st, inc. *34 sts*

Row 9: Inc, k1, p2, C4F, p2, k2, p2, k6, p2, k2, p2, C4F, p2, k1, inc. *36 sts*

Row 11: Inc, k2, p2, k4, p2, k2, p2, C6F, p2, k2, p2, k4, p2, k2, inc. *38 sts*

Row 13: Inc, work every st in patt as it presents to last st, inc. *40 sts*

Row 15: Inc, p2, k2, p2, C4F, p2, k2, p2, k6, p2, k2, p2, C4F, p2, k2, p2, inc. *42 sts*

Row 17: Inc, work every st in patt as it presents to last st, inc. *44 sts*

Row 19: Inc, work every st in patt as it presents to last st, inc. *46 sts*

Row 21: Inc, k3, p2, k2, p2, C4F, p2, k2, p2, C4F, p2, k2, p2, C4F, p2, k2, p2, k3, inc. *48 sts*

Row 23: Inc, work every st in patt as it presents to last st, inc. *50 sts*

Row 25: Inc, work every st in patt as it presents to last st, inc. *52 sts*

Row 27: Inc, k6, p2, k2, p2, C4F, p2, k2, p2, k6, p2, k2, p2, C4F, p2, k2, p2, k6, inc. *54 sts*

Row 29: Work every st in patt as it presents.

Row 31: P2, k6, p2, k2, p2, k4, p2, k2, p2, C6F, p2, k2, p2, k4, p2, k2, p2, k6, p2.

Row 33: P2, k6, p2, k2, p2, C4F, p2, k2, p2, k6, p2, k2, p2, C4F, p2, k2, p2, k6, p2.

Row 35: Work every st in patt as it presents.

Row 37: P1, skpo, work every st in patt as it presents to last 3 sts, k2tog, p1. *52 sts*

Row 39: P1, skpo, k4, p2, k2, p2, C4F, p2, k2, p2, k6, p2, k2, p2, C4F, p2, k2, p2, k4, k2tog, p1. *50 sts*

Row 41: K1, skpo, k3, p2, k2, p2, k4, p2, k2, p2, C6F, p2, k2, p2, k4, p2, k2, p2, k3, k2tog, k1. *48 sts*

Row 43: K1, skpo, work every st in patt as it presents to last 3 sts, k2tog, k1. *46 sts*

Row 45: K1, skpo, k1, p2, k2, p2, C4F, p2, k2, p2, k6, p2, k2, p2, C4F, p2, k2, p2, k1, k2tog, k1. *44 sts*

Row 47: K1, skpo, work every st in patt as it presents to last 3 sts, k2tog, k1. *42 sts*

Row 49: K1, sppo, work every st in patt as it presents to last 3 sts, p2tog, k1. *40 sts*

Row 51: K1, sppo, k2, p2, C4F, p2, k2, p2, C6F, p2, k2, p2, C4F, p2, k2, p2tog, k1. *38 sts*

Row 53: P1, skpo, work every st in patt as it presents to last 3 sts, k2tog, p1. *36 sts*

Row 55: K1, skpo, work every st in patt as it presents to last 3 sts, k2tog, k1. *34 sts*

Row 57: K1, sppo, p1, C4F, p2, k2, p2, k6, p2, k2, p2, C4F, p1, p2tog, k1. *32 sts*

Row 59: K1, sppo, work every st in patt as it presents to last 3 sts, p2tog, k1. *30 sts*

Row 61: P1, skpo, work every st in patt as it presents to last 3 sts, k2tog, p1. *28 sts*

Row 63: Work every st in patt as it presents.
Bind (cast) off.

TO MAKE UP
- Weave in all loose ends.
- Carefully use the craft knife to cut a ¼in (0.5cm) hole in the center of the board. Cut the foam into a circle 1in (2.5cm) larger than the cake board and wrap it over edge, gluing it in place on the back.
- Using a running stitch, lace a strong string around the edge of the knitting. Stretch the knitting over the front of the covered board, then pull the string tight on the back and secure it with a firm double knot.
- Cut the fabric into a circle the same size as the clock. Turn under the edge by ⅜in (1cm) all around. Sew the fabric in place, covering the edge of the knitting, with sewing thread and hemming stitch.
- Cut a small hole in the backing fabric and attach the clock mechanism through the hole in the board, following the manufacturer's instructions.

changing direction
When you make up the clock, choose the angle you want the cables to run in. They can point directly from 12 to 6, or slant across at a quirky angle.

chunky knit rug

This knitted rug creates a warm and cozy atmosphere and is wonderfully soft underfoot. You soon get used to handling the giant knitting needles and they make the knitting "grow" incredibly quickly.

Skill level ✳

Size
Approx. 39 x 38½in (100 x 98cm)

Materials
YARN
Felted wool yarn such as Dreadlock Wool from Texere—100% wool; approx. 175yds (160m) per 4lb 8oz (2kg) cone
- Ecru—approx. 4lb 8oz (2kg)/ 175yds (160m)

NEEDLES
Pair of 1½in (4cm) knitting needles (see Resources, page 126)

OTHER MATERIALS
- Tapestry needle

Gauge (tension)
3 sts and 4.5 rows to 4in (10cm) over st st using 1½in (4cm) needles

Abbreviations
See page 124

Pattern
MAIN PIECE
Cast on 30 sts.
Row 1: P2 [k2, p2] to end.
Rows 2–8: Work every st in 2x2 rib patt as it presents.
Beg with a k row, work 26 rows st st.
Rep rows 1–8.
Bind (cast) off.

TO FINISH
- Weave in all loose ends. Press the knitting flat following the instructions on the yarn wrapper.

Changing size
This pattern will make a perfect bedside rug. To make a larger rug, simply add more rows into the stockinette stitch section.

equipment & techniques

On the following pages you'll find instructions for all the knitting and crochet skills you'll need in order to make any of the projects.

basic knitting equipment

The projects in this book require only the simplest tools to make them.

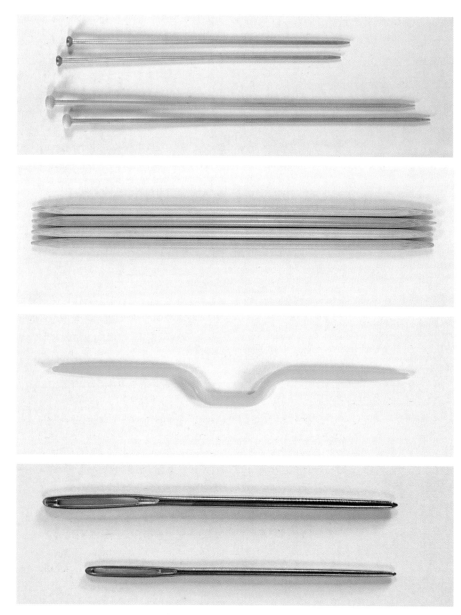

Single-point knitting needles come in various sizes and materials. The size required is given in each pattern, but the material is a personal choice for the knitter. Beginners often find bamboo needles easiest because they are less slippery than metal or plastic knitting needles.

Double-pointed knitting needles (DPNs) are used in sets of four or five (sets of four are fine for the projects in this book) and allow you to knit off both ends in order to knit in the round (see page 113).

A cable needle is used to hold a group of stitches at the front or back of the work while working a cable twist (see pages 110–111). The size should correspond with the size of knitting needles being used. You can get cranked cable needles, like this one, which are easier to use than straight cable needles if you are a beginner knitter.

A tapestry needle is used to sew together pieces of knitting (see page 114). These needles have blunt ends to help prevent them splitting the yarn.

knitting techniques

For beginner knitters the following pages will show you all the techniques you need to get you started with the simpler projects in this book. Master how to cast on, form knit and purl stitches, and bind (cast) off, before moving onto cabling and shaping (they are easier than you might think once you're familiar with the basics).

Holding needles and yarn

Every knitter will develop their own style, but there are two popular ways to hold the knitting needles. Try them both and adopt the style that feels more natural for you.

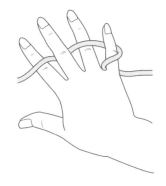

RIGHT HAND LIKE A KNIFE

Pick up the needles in both hands as you would a knife and fork, with the needles running under the palms of your hands. You will need to let go of the knitting with your right hand—tuck the blunt end of the needle under your arm to hold it—in order to move the yarn around the tip of the needle.

RIGHT HAND LIKE A PEN

Keeping the left hand in the same position, hold the right-hand needle as you would hold a pen, with the needle resting in the crook of your hand. This position has the advantage that you can control the yarn with your right index finger without letting go of the needles.

HOLDING THE YARN

In order to create even knitting the yarn will need to be tensioned. You can wrap the yarn differently around your fingers depending on your natural gauge (tension), but try this method first because it works for most people.

Wind the yarn around your little finger and lace it over the ring finger, under the second finger and over the first finger. The right-hand index finger will be used to wind the yarn around the needle point.

Slip knot

Every piece of knitting starts with a simple slip knot.

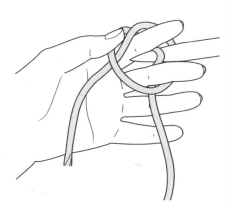

1 Leaving about a 4in (10cm) tail of yarn, wind yarn twice around two fingers of your left hand. Slip the tip of a knitting needle between your fore and second fingers and under the loop furthest from the fingertips, as shown. Draw this loop through the other loop.

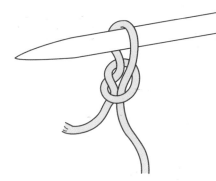

2 Pull on the ends of the yarn to tighten the loop on the needle; this has created the first stitch.

Casting on (cable method)

I usually use the cable method to cast on stitches: this technique can be used in all projects in this book and creates a neat, firm edge.

1 Hold needle with slip knot in your left hand. Insert the tip of the right-hand needle from left to right into the front of the knot.

2 *Wrap the yarn under and around the tip of the right-hand needle.

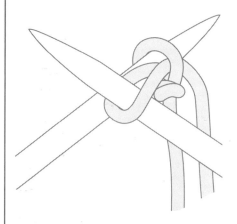

3 Draw the yarn through to form a new stitch on the right-hand needle.

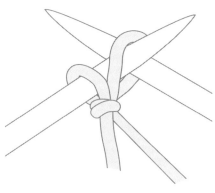

4 Slip this stitch from the right-hand needle onto the left-hand needle.

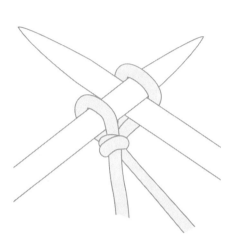

5 For every following stitch, insert the right-hand needle between the two previous stitches.

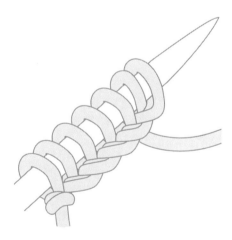

6 Repeat from * until you have the required number of stitches on the left-hand needle.

EXTRA STITCHES

To cast on extra stitches in the middle of a project, repeat from step 5.

Knit stitch

This is the first and easiest stitch that a beginner will learn. Rows of knit stitches create garter stitch. The yarn should be held at the back of the work.

1 Hold the needle with the cast-on stitches in your left hand. Insert the right-hand needle into the front of the first stitch, from left to right (this is called "knitwise"), and take the yarn under and around the tip.

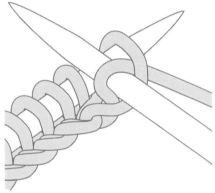

2 Use the tip of the right-hand needle to draw the loop through the stitch.

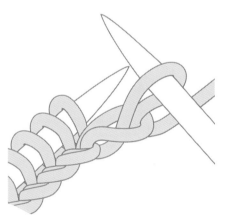

3 Slip the original stitch off the left-hand needle to complete the first knit stitch. Repeat these three steps until all the stitches on the left-hand needle have been transferred to the right-hand needle. At the end of the row, swap the needles so that all the stitches are again in your left hand.

Purl stitch

This is the only other basic stitch to master. A row of knit stitch followed by a row of purl stitch creates stockinette (stocking) stitch. The yarn should be held at the front of the work.

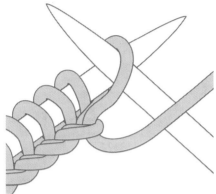

1 Hold the needle with the cast-on stitches in your left hand. Insert the right-hand needle into the front of the first stitch, from right to left (this is called "purlwise").

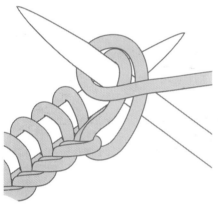

2 Take the yarn over and around the tip of the right-hand needle.

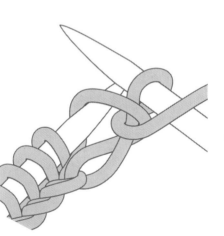

3 Use the tip of the right-hand needle to draw the loop through the stitch. Slip the original stitch off the left-hand needle to complete the first purl stitch.
Repeat these three steps until all the stitches on the left-hand needle have been transferred to the right-hand needle. At the end of the row, swap the needles so that all the stitches are again in your left hand.

Binding (casting) off

This is done to secure the final edge of the knitting so that it will not come undone. If you have been working a stitch pattern (see page 112), then work each stitch as it presents, so knit a knit stitch and purl a purl stitch as you bind (cast) off.

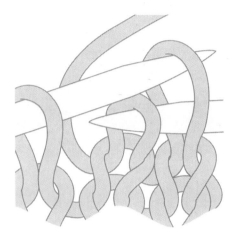

1 Work the first two stitches. *Insert the tip of the left-hand needle into the first stitch on the right-hand needle and lift this stitch over the second stitch and off the needle. Work the next stitch on the left-hand needle so that there are again two stitches on the right-hand needle*. Repeat from * until only one stitch remains.

2 Cut the yarn leaving a 4in (10cm) tail and slip the final stitch off the needle. Draw the tail through the stitch and pull the tail to tighten the stitch.

Shaping

Through increasing and decreasing the number of stitches you can shape a piece of knitting. Different methods are used because they make the stitches slope in different directions to create a neater look.

Increasing

This involves creating new stitches in a row to make the knitting wider. There are three methods of increasing that appear in the projects in this book.

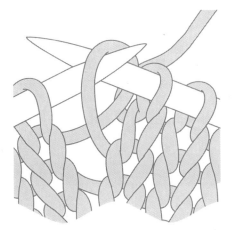

MAKE ONE (m1)

Insert the tip of the left-hand needle under the front of the horizontal strand lying between the last stitch and the next stitch. Lift this strand and knit into the back of it in order to make a new stitch. Knitting into the back twists the loop and stops a hole appearing where you have increased.

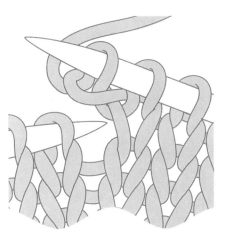

INCREASE (inc)

Knit the stitch in the usual way, but without dropping the original stitch off the left-hand needle. Now knit into the back of the same stitch and drop the original off the left-hand needle as usual. You are creating a new stitch by knitting one stitch twice.

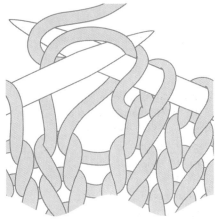

YARNOVER (yo)

Create an extra stitch by passing the yarn over the right-hand needle between stitches. When knitting, bring the yarn between the point of the two needles, then over the right-hand needle and to the back, ready to knit the next stitch, as shown here. When purling, wrap the yarn all the way around the needle so that it comes back in front where it needs to be to purl the next stitch. On the next row, treat this new stitch in the same way as all other stitches.

Decreasing

This involves reducing the number of stitches in a row to make the knitting narrower. There are several methods of decreasing used in this book.

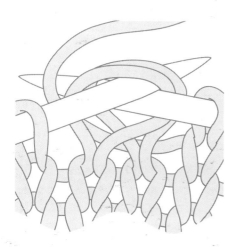

KNIT TWO TOGETHER (k2tog)

Insert the right-hand needle knitwise through the front of the next two stitches on the left-hand needle and knit them together as though they were one stitch. Slip both stitches off the left-hand needle, leaving one stitch on the right-hand needle.

PURL TWO TOGETHER (p2tog)

Insert the right-hand needle purlwise through the front of the next two stitches on the left-hand needle and purl them together as though they were one stitch. Slip both stitches off the left-hand needle, leaving one stitch on the right-hand needle.

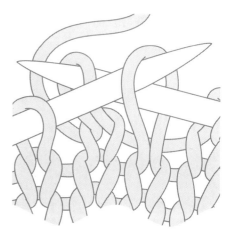

SLIP ONE, KNIT ONE, PASS THE SLIPPED STITCH OVER (skpo)

Insert the right-hand needle knitwise into the next stitch and slip it directly onto that needle, without actually knitting it. Knit the next stitch as usual. Using the tip of the left-hand needle, lift the slipped stitch over the knitted one and drop it off the right-hand needle.

SLIP ONE, PURL ONE, PASS THE SLIPPED STITCH OVER (sppo)

This is the same principle as skpo (see above), but worked on a purl row. Insert the right-hand needle purlwise into the next stitch and slip it directly onto that needle, without actually purling it. Purl the next stitch as usual. Using the tip of the left-hand needle, lift the slipped stitch over the purled one and drop it off the right-hand needle.

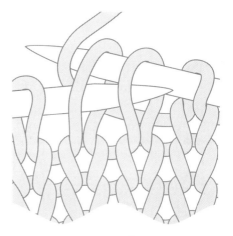

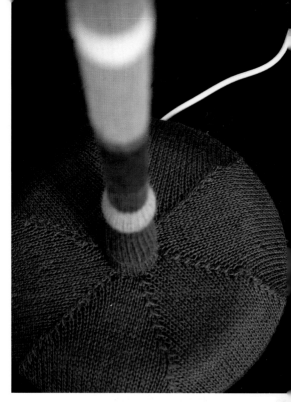

SLIP ONE, SLIP ONE , KNIT TWO TOGETHER (ssk)

Insert the right-hand needle knitwise into the next stitch and slip it directly onto that needle, without actually knitting it. Do the same again so that you have slipped two stitches. Insert the tip of the left-hand needle through the front of both stitches, from left to right as shown, and knit them together as one stitch.

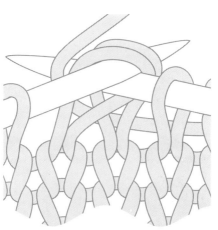

SLIP ONE, KNIT TWO TOGETHER, PASS THE SLIPPED STITCH OVER (sk2po)

1 This decreases the stitch number by two rather than just one. Insert the right-hand needle knitwise into the next stitch and slip it directly onto that needle, without actually knitting it. Knit the next two stitches together (see k2tog, opposite).

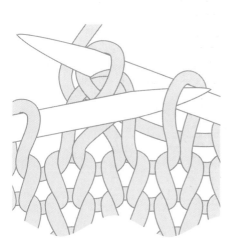

2 Using the tip of the left-hand needle, lift the slipped stitch over the k2tog and drop it off the right-hand needle.

Cables

Create texture and pattern by swapping the order in which you knit stitches. Cables are much simpler to work than you might at first think, and using a bent cable needle (see page 100) will make it even easier to hold the group of stitches being moved.

CABLE FOUR FORWARD (C4F)

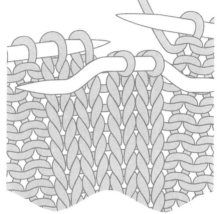

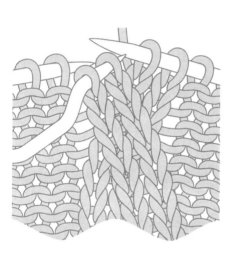

CABLE FOUR FORWARD (C4F)

1 Work to the position of the cable. Slip the next two stitches on the left-hand needle onto the cable needle and hold it at the front of the work.

2 Knit the next two stitches off the left-hand needle in the usual way, then knit the two stitches off the cable needle.

CABLE SIX FORWARD (C6F)

As above, but hold three stitches at the front on the cable needle.

CABLE EIGHT FORWARD (C8F)

As above, but hold four stitches at the front on the cable needle.

CABLE TEN FORWARD (C10F)

As above, but hold five stitches at the front on the cable needle.

CABLE FOUR BACK (C4B)

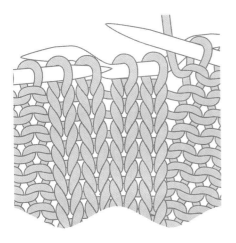

1 Work to the position of the cable. Slip the next two stitches on the left-hand needle onto the cable needle and hold it at the back of the work.

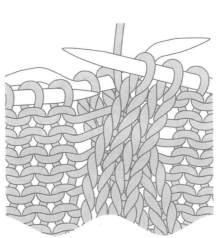

2 Knit the next two stitches off the left-hand needle in the usual way, then knit the two stitches off the cable needle.

CABLE THREE LEFT (C3L)

Work to the position of the cable. Slip the next two stitches on the left-hand needle onto the cable needle and hold it at the front of the work. Purl the next stitch off the left-hand needle in the usual way, then knit the two stitches off the cable needle.

CABLE THREE RIGHT (C3R)

Work to the position of the cable. Slip the next stitch on the left-hand needle onto the cable needle and hold it at the back of the work. Knit the next two stitches off the left-hand needle in the usual way, then purl the single stitch off the cable needle.

Working in pattern

You will find the phrase "work every st in patt as it presents" in many patterns in this book, and it means that you need to work the stitches in the pattern set on previous rows.

The simplest way to understand this is that if the next stitch on the left-hand needle looks like a knit stitch (it is a V shape), then you should knit it. If it looks like a purl stitch (it is a little bump), then you should purl it. Once you've worked a couple of rows, the stitch pattern will be established and will be easy to see.

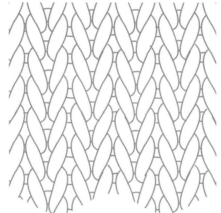

Stockinette (stocking) stitch is made by knitting and purling entire alternate rows.

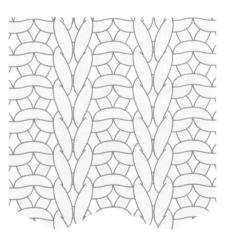

Rib is made by knitting and purling alternate stitches on every row; working each stitch as it presents will create columns of knit and purl stitches.

Knitting in the round

This is a method of knitting using double-pointed needles to work continuously around the stitches to create a seamless tube.

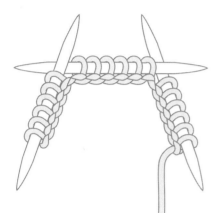

1 Cast on the required number of stitches onto one double-pointed needle. Slip some stitches from either end onto two more needles so that there are an equal number of stitches on three needles. Check that the stitches all lie flat and that this cast-on row is not twisted.

2 Use a stitch marker, or a loop of contrast yarn: this marker will just be passed from one needle to another to mark the start of each round. Using the fourth needle, knit the first cast-on stitch, pulling the yarn tightly so that the three original needles form a triangle. Knit all the stitches off the first needle. Using this newly free needle, knit all the stitches off the second needle, and then knit them all off the third. Once you have knitted all the stitches off all three needles in turn, you have completed one round of knitting.

Picking up stitches

In order to continue knitting but in a different direction, you need to pick up stitches along a side edge of a completed piece of knitting.

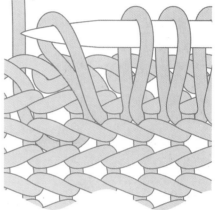

With the right side of the work facing you, insert a knitting needle into the knitted fabric between the edge stitch and the next stitch along on the first row. Wrap the yarn knitwise around the tip of the needle. Pull through a loop, so creating a new stitch on the knitting needle. Repeat the process along the edge to pick up the required number of stitches, making sure you space them evenly.

To make up

It's important to finish and sew up your projects as carefully as you knitted them for a good-looking result. Mattress stitch is worked on the right side of the knitting and allows you to perfectly match a stitch pattern or stripes.

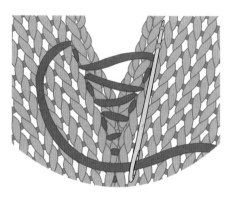

LOOSE ENDS

Weave in the tails of yarn from casting on and binding (casting) off to create a neat and secure finish. Using a tapestry needle, sew the tail up and down through the backs of at least five stitches across a row. Do not pull the tail tight or the knitting will pucker.

MATTRESS STITCH ON CAST ON AND BOUND (CAST) OFF EDGES

Lay the two pieces right-side up with the edges to be joined touching. Thread a tapestry needle with a length of the project yarn (or yarn in a matching color if the project yarn is not very strong). Secure the yarn on the back of the upper piece, at one end of the seam. Bring yarn through to the front between the first and second stitch of the first row. Insert the needle between the first and second stitch of the first row on the other piece. Pass the needle under both strands of the second stitch and back through to the front. Insert the needle into the same hole it emerged from on the first piece and pass it under both strands of the second stitch and back through to the front. Repeat this process, zig-zagging from one piece to the other and always taking the needle under both strands of the next stitch along. After every two or three stitches, pull up the yarn gently to close the seam.

MATTRESS STITCH ON ROW ENDS

Lay the two pieces right-side up with the edges to be joined touching. Secure the yarn on the back of the right-hand piece, at the bottom of the seam. Bring yarn through to the front between the first and second stitch of the first row. Insert the needle between the first and second stitch of the first row on the other piece. Pass the needle upward, under the horizontal strand of yarn between the first and second stitch, then under the same strand in the row above, and bring it through back to the front. Insert the needle into the same hole it emerged from on the first piece and pass it upward under the corresponding horizontal strands. Repeat this process, zig-zagging from one side to the other and always taking the needle under two horizontal strands. After every two or three stitches, pull up the yarn gently to close the seam.

trouble shooting

A dropped stitch may feel like a disaster, but if caught in time it is easy to correct.

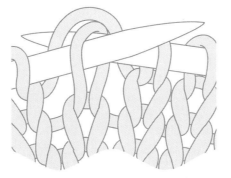

HOLDING A STITCH

Keep a safety pin or a stitch holder pinned to the top of your knitting project bag so that it's to hand in case of a dropped stitch emergency. Put the pin or holder through the stitch loop as soon as you can to stop it unraveling any further while you get ready to pick it up.

PICKING UP A STITCH DROPPED IN THE ROW YOU ARE KNITTING

Insert the right-hand needle into the loop of the dropped stitch and under the strand it has dropped from. Use the tip of the left-hand needle to pass the stitch over the strand, dropping the stitch and pulling the loop of the strand through. Ensure that the stitch is lying on the left-hand needle and is facing in the correct direction, then continue knitting.

PICKING UP A DROPPED STITCH FROM SEVERAL ROWS BELOW

Insert a crochet hook into the loop of the dropped stitch at the bottom of the ladder that has appeared. Catch the strand lying directly above it and draw this strand through the loop. Continue in this way up the ladder until all the strands have been caught, then slip the final loop onto the left-hand needle.

crochet techniques

Simple crochet has been used in several projects in this book. Here are instructions for the required techniques.

Holding the work

As for knitting, there are different ways of holding the hook and yarn; this is the most popular way.

Hold the hook in your right hand and grip the slip knot between the finger and thumb of your left hand. Wind the yarn around your little finger and over the other fingers of your left hand to tension it. As you progress, always pinch the work just below the stitch that you are working on to hold it.

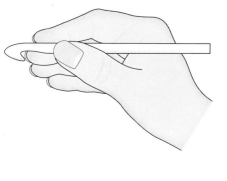

Making a chain

Always start with a slip knot around the crochet hook; this does not count as the first chain.

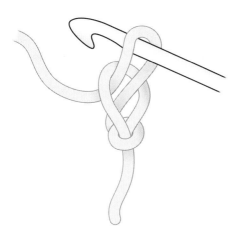

Dip the tip of the hook to catch the yarn and draw it back through the slip knot to make one chain. Repeat, drawing the caught yarn through the previous chain loop each time until the required number of chains have been made.

Terms used in these techniques and in the crochet patterns for the Knitted Vase Cozy (see page 16), Corsage Coat Hooks (see page 20), and the Curtain Tie (see page 90) are US crochet terms. The equivalent UK terms are listed here.

USA – American English	British English
single crochet (sc)	double crochet (dc)
half double crochet (hdc)	half treble (htr)
double crochet (dc)	treble (tr)
treble (tr)	double treble (dtr)
double treble (dtr)	triple treble (trtr)
skip	miss
gauge	tension
yarn over (yo)	yarn over hook (yoh)
slip stitch (sl st)	slip stitch (ss)

Slip stitch (sl st)

This is used to join a chain into a circle, or to move along a crocheted edge without adding stitch height.

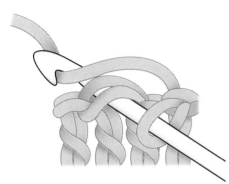

Insert the hook into the chain as instructed. Catch the yarn and draw a loop through the stitch and through the loop on the hook.

Single crochet (sc)

This is the simplest crochet stitch.

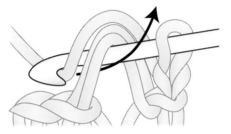

1 Insert the hook into the chain, or into the stitch on the previous row, as instructed. Wrap the yarn over the hook and draw it through the stitch only, making two loops on the hook.

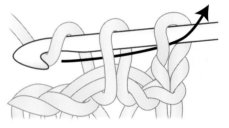

2 Catch the yarn and draw a loop through both loops on the hook.

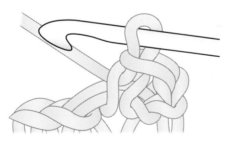

3 One loop remains on the hook and the stitch is complete.

Double crochet (dc)

For a longer crochet stitch, more loops are made on the hook.

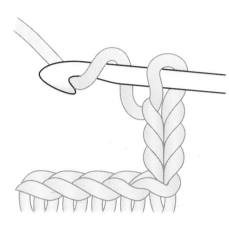

1 Wrap the yarn around the hook. Insert the hook into the chain, or into the stitch on the previous row, as instructed.

3 Catch the yarn and draw a loop through the first two loops on the hook, making two loops on the hook.

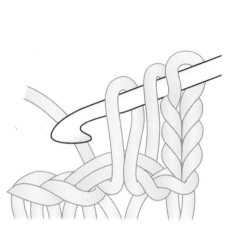

2 Catch the yarn and draw a loop through the stitch only, making three loops on the hook.

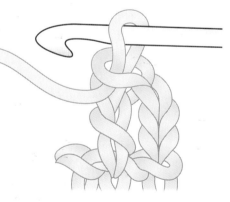

4 Catch the yarn again and draw a loop through the two loops on the hook so that just one loop remains.

Treble crochet (tr)

This follows the same principle as double crochet in that a loop is drawn through two loops on the hook each time.

Wrap the yarn twice around the hook. Insert the hook into the chain of the first row, or into the stitch directly below for every following row. Catch the yarn and draw a loop through the stitch only, making four loops on the hook. Catch the yarn and draw a loop through the first two loops, making three loops on the hook. Catch the yarn again and draw a loop through the next two loops, making two loops on the hook. Catch the yarn again and draw a loop through the final two loops so you are left with just one loop on the hook.

Fastening off

The first method is the most usual way of fastening off and is the most secure. The second method makes a neat finish, especially when working motifs.

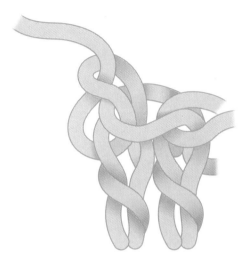

First method: After the last stitch pull another loop through, cut the yarn, and pull the end through the loop.

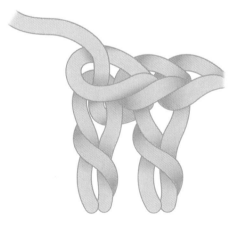

Second method: After the last stitch cut the yarn and pull the end through. Darn in the end very securely.

gauge (tension)

To ensure that your finished knitting is the correct size, it is imperative to knit a gauge (tension) swatch that you can check against the details given in the pattern you have chosen. The gauge is given as the number of stitches in a 4 × 4in (10 × 10cm) square.

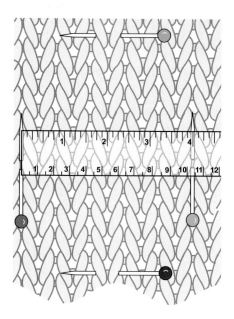

- Using the recommended yarn and needles, cast on eight stitches more than the gauge (tension) instruction asks for (so if you need to have 10 stitches to 4in (10cm), cast on 18 stitches). Working in pattern as instructed, work eight rows more than is needed. Bind (cast) off loosely.
- Lay the swatch flat without stretching it (the gauge is given before washing or felting). Lay a ruler across the stitches with the 2in (5cm) mark centered on the knitting, then put a pin in the knitting at the start of the ruler and at the 4in (10cm) mark: the pins should be well away from the edges of the swatch. Count the number of stitches between the pins. Repeat the process across the rows to count the number of rows to 4in (10cm).
- If the number of stitches and rows you've counted is the same as the number asked for in the instructions, you have the correct gauge (tension). If you do not have the same number then you will need to change your gauge (tension). Don't just try to knit to a different gauge (tension): everyone has a "natural" gauge (tension) and if you try to knit tighter or looser it won't be consistent and you will simply end up with uneven knitting. To change gauge (tension) you

need to change the size of your knitting needles. A good rule of thumb to follow is that one difference in needle size will create a difference of one stitch in the gauge (tension). You will need to use larger needles to achieve fewer stitches and smaller ones to achieve more stitches, so if you have one too many stitches, knit another swatch with needles one size larger. If you have one too few stitches, use needles one size smaller.
- Work swatches until you have the right gauge (tension): it might seem a bit time-consuming, but it's better then knitting a whole project and than finding out that it's the wrong size.

substituting yarn

If you want to change the yarn, then you need to work out how many balls to buy.

- Choose a substitute yarn that is the same thickness as the pattern yarn or you'll end up with a project that's an entirely different size. Balls of two different brands of the same type of yarn won't necessarily contain the same quantity of yarn, even if the balls weigh the same. It's the yardage (meterage) in a ball, not the weight that's important.
- And different yarns may not knit up to the same gauge (tension). The yarn wrapper on the substitute yarn should give you its standard gauge (tension), and as long as this isn't different from the pattern yarn gauge (tension) by more than a stitch or row, or two, you should be able to get the right gauge (tension) (see opposite).

- Before buying all the substitute yarn, buy just one ball and knit a gauge (tension) swatch to be absolutely certain that you can get the right gauge (tension) with that yarn.
- If the substitute yarn has a different yardage (meterage) per ball to the pattern yarn, then you need to do a sum to work out how many balls to buy.
- Multiply the yardage (meterage) in one ball of pattern yarn by the number of balls needed to find out the total yardage (meterage) of yarn required.
- Then divide the total yardage (meterage) by the yardage (meterage) in one ball of the substitute yarn to find out how many balls of that yarn you need to buy.

Example:
The pattern yarn has 109yds (100m) of yarn in each ball and you need 13 balls.
109 (100) x 13 = 1417yds (1300m) of yarn needed in total.

The substitute yarn has 123yds (112m) of yarn in each ball.
1417 ÷ 123 = 11.52
(1300 ÷ 112 = 11.6)
So you only need to buy 12 balls of the substitute yarn.

felting the knitting

There are three factors needed for a felted finish: water, temperature change, and agitation. Washing detergent aids the process.

- Fill one basin with cold water and another with water as hot as it will come from the tap (wear rubber gloves to protect your hands when using the hot water). Add a small amount of handwash detergent to the hot basin.
- Plunge the knitting to be felted into the hot water and rub it vigorously against itself.

- Dunk the knitting in and out of the hot water several times, and change your grip on it regularly so that the felting happens evenly across the work.
- Every so often, plunge the knit into the cold water to shock the fibers; this shock helps the wool to felt.
- Continue in this way until the knitting is felted to the required amount.

- Rinse out all the detergent residue and spin or squeeze the knitting dry. Leave to dry flat for a minimum of 12 hours.
- If when you have dried your knitting you find that you have not felted it quite enough, you can repeat this felting process until you get the result you require.

making up knitted pieces

The projects are straightforward to make up—and there are clear instructions on how to sew them—but there are a couple of projects where illustrations may help you.

Knitted Upright Chair
(see page 10)

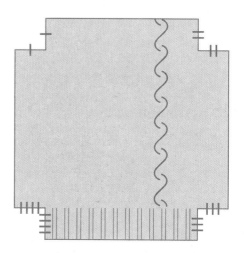

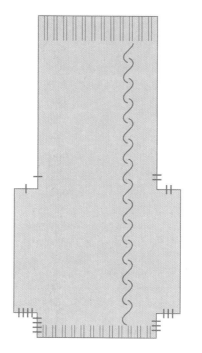

Cable Trim Wastebasket
(see page 84)

CHAIR SEAT
- Using mattress stitch (see page 114), sew the sections with matching marks together to create a box shape that will slip over the seat pad of the chair. The same principle applies to sewing up the Color Block Footstool (see page 30).

CHAIR BACK
- The same principle applies to the chair back, but the long flap that will cover the back of the chair back is initially left loose. Fit the knitting over the chair back pad, pin the back flap in place to the edges of the side and bottom pieces, then sew the seams using mattress stitch (see page 114).

- This illustration will also help you understand where to pick up stitches along the sides of the base square.
- When sewing up, each cable partly overlaps the plain edge of the adjacent side piece, so that the cables themselves run up the corners of the wastebasket.

measuring furniture and calculating patterns

It is very likely that a piece of furniture you want to cover will be a slightly different size to a piece I have covered in this book, but these are not complicated patterns and so it's not difficult to adjust them; you just need to do the math.

- First, knit an accurate gauge (tension) square (see page 120); it's vital that you do this or your sums won't work out.
- Measure the width of pad to be covered, this should include 1in (2.5cm) underneath at either side: so measure, 1in (2.5cm) + height of pad + across top of pad + height of pad + 1in (2.5cm). This measurement is the required width of the knitting.
- To calculate how many stitches to cast on, divide the pad measurement by 4 (10), rounding up to the nearest whole number, then multiply that figure by the number of stitches to 4in (10cm) in your gauge (tension) swatch.

Example:
If pad measurement is 27½in (70cm)
And the gauge (tension) is 19 stitches to 4in (10cm)
Divide 27½ (70) by 4 (10) = 7
7 x 19 = 133 stitches to cast on.

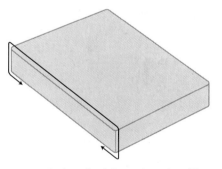

Measure the length of the pad, again adding 1in (2.5cm) underneath on each side, and repeat the process to calculate how many rows to work.
Example:
If pad measurement is 27½in (70cm)
And the gauge (tension) is 25 rows to 4in (10cm)
Divide 27½ (70) by 4 (10) = 7
7 x 25 = 175 rows to work.

Abbreviations

approx	approximately	rev st st	reverse stockinette (stocking) stitch
alt	alternate; alternatively	RH	right-hand
beg	begin(s)(ning)	RS	right side
C4B	cable four stitches (or number stated) back	sc	single crochet
C4F	cable four stitches (or number stated) front	sl2p	slip 2 stitches purlwise
ch	chain	sl st	slip stitch
cm	centimeters	skpo	slip 1, knit 1, pass slipped stitch over
cont	continue	sk2po	slip one stitch, knit two together, pass slipped stitch over
dc	double crochet		
DK	double knitting	sppo	slip 1, purl 1, pass slipped stitch over
g	gram(s)	ssk	slip one stitch, slip one stitch, knit the slipped stitches together
inc	increase		
k	knit		
k2tog	knit two stitches (or number stated) together	st(s)	stitch(es)
LH	left-hand	st st	stockinette (stocking) stitch
m	meters	tog	together
m1	make 1 stitch	tr	treble crochet
mm	millimeters	WS	wrong side
oz	ounce(es)	wyb	with yarn at back
p	purl	wyf	with yarn in front
p2tog	purl two stitches (or number stated) together	yo	yarn over
rem	remain(ing)	[ ]	repeat instructions inside [ ] as given
rep	repeat	* *	repeat instructions between * * as given

Knitting needle sizes

There are three systems of sizing knitting needles, and not every size exists in every system.
This chart compares sizes across the three systems.

US	Metric	old UK and Canadian	US	Metric	old UK and Canadian
50	25mm	–	8	5mm	6
35	19mm	–	7	4.5mm	7
19	15mm	–	6	4mm	8
17	12mm	–	5	3.75mm	9
15	10mm	000	4	3.5mm	–
13	9mm	00	3	3.25mm	10
11	8mm	0	2/3	3mm	11
11	7.5mm	1	2	2.75mm	12
10½	7mm	2	1	2.25mm	13
10½	6.5mm	3	0	2mm	14
10	6mm	4	00	1.75mm	–
9	5.5mm	5	000	1.5mm	–

Yarn standards

The Yarn Council of America offers the following system of categorizing yarns, and you might find it useful. However, it really is only a general guide and if you are knitting from a pattern you should use the gauge (tension) and needle sizes that it suggests, as those are what the designer has used to create the project.

Yarn weight symbol	Yarn category names	Suggested US (metric) needle size	Gauge range in stockinette (stocking) stitch over 4in (10cm)
0 LACE	fingering, 4-ply, 10-count crochet thread	000–1 (1.5–2.25mm)	33–40 sts
1 SUPER FINE	fingering, 4-ply, sock, baby	1–2 (2.25–3.25mm)	27–32 sts
2 FINE	light-weight double knitting, sport-weight, baby	3–5 (3.25–3.75mm)	23–26 sts
3 LIGHT	light-weight worsted, double knitting	5–7 (3.75–4.5mm)	21–24 sts
4 MEDIUM	worsted, afghan, Aran	7–9 (4.5–5.5mm)	16–20 sts
5 BULKY	chunky, craft, rug	9–11 (5.5–8mm)	12–15 sts
6 SUPER BULKY	bulky, roving, super-chunky	11 and larger (8mm and larger)	6–11 sts

Weights and lengths

You can use either the metric or imperial measurement system in a project, but don't mix the two. This chart tells you how to convert from one system to another.

ounces = grams x 0.0352

grams = ounces x 28.35

inches = centimeters x 0.3937

centimeters = inches x 2.54

yards = meters x 0.9144

meters = yards x 1.0936

resources

Melanie Porter can be contacted at info@melanieporter.co.uk or visit her website at www.melanieporter.co.uk

Yarns (UK and US)
Texere Yarns Ltd
College Mill
Barkerend Road
Bradford BD1 4AU
www.texere-yarns.co.uk

Rowan
Green Lane Mill
Holmfirth
West Yorkshire HD9 2DX
www.knitrowan.com

Giant knitting needles
Made to measure by Michael Williams
www.michael-williams-wood.co.uk

SPECIFIC PROJECT MATERIALS

Below is a list of suppliers that I used for the projects included in this book. Many of these materials can be sourced from local craft and hardware stores or easily found online.

Small Bell Lampshade and Color Block Lampshade (see pages 13 and 38)
Lampshade 6in (15cm) high with top diameter of 3½in (9cm) and bottom diameter of 8⅛in (20.5cm)
The Internet Electrical Store
www.theinternetelectricalstore.com

Flower Vase Cozy (see page 16)
6in (15cm) vase
Ikea
www.ikea.com

Rope Knit Basket (see page 18)
12in (30cm) round, plywood basket base
Great Art
www.greatart.co.uk

Basket Bases by Rusty
www.basketbasesbyrusty.com

Stripe Knit Clock and Cable Clock (see pages 26 and 92)
Clock mechanism
Clock Parts
www.clockparts.co.uk

Clockworks
www.clockworks.com

Colour Block Footstool (see page 30)
Queen Anne-style footstool
Ebay, from walesuphol

Stripe Drum Lampshade (see page 41)
12in (30cm) fabric-lined drum lampshade
Homebase
www.homebase.co.uk

Amazon
www.amazon.com

Cable Trim Wastebasket (see page 64)
Square wastebasket measuring 10¼in (26cm) high by 10in (25cm) square on the top edge and 6in (15cm) square on the bottom edge
John Lewis
www.johnlewis.com

Cable Lampshade (see page 70)
16in (40cm) coolie lampshade
The Internet Electrical Store
www.theinternetelectricalstore.com

Cable Vase Cuff (see page 78)
7in (18cm) vase
Ikea
www.ikea.com

Knitted Wall Hearts (see page 84)
Heart-shaped box
Hobby Craft
www.hobbycraft.co.uk

index

acknowledgments

There are many people without whom I never would have been able to complete this book. Firstly, thank you to Cindy Richards and the team at CICO Books for commissioning this book, and to Carmel Edmonds with her endless patience and for responding to countless questions. Thanks to Marilyn Wilson for tireless pattern checking, and Kate Haxell for help and suggestions during editing.

Thank you to Emma Mitchell and Tanya Goodwin for creating such fantastic photography.

Thanks to Daisy James for her help with the patterns, and a huge thank you to my mum who spends many hours knitting for me.

And finally thank you to my partner, Vik, for his patience with my knitting endlessly into the night, and for putting up with yarn and knitting permanently drying in the bathroom.

Rowan Yarns and Texere Yarns kindly supplied fantastic yarns for me to work with.